JOHN COTTON DANA

JOHN COTTON DANA
A Life

BY FRANK KINGDON
PRESIDENT OF THE UNIVERSITY OF NEWARK

Newark

THE PUBLIC LIBRARY AND MUSEUM

1940

D. B. Updike, The Merrymount Press, Boston, U. S. A.

THIS LIFE OF JOHN COTTON DANA
IS DEDICATED
TO
BEATRICE WINSER
HIS COLLEAGUE AND SUCCESSOR
IN THE WORK OF BOTH
THE NEWARK PUBLIC LIBRARY
AND
THE NEWARK MUSEUM

PREFACE

Before I had been in Newark very long I realized that its civic and cultural life had been more tangibly moulded by the work and character of one man than by any other. Because I strongly believe that no community can afford to forget its best men and because part of the strengthening of a city is the building of its tradition, I have written this book. It will be of interest not only to the people of the community that he served so ably, but also to the profession of which he was a recognized leader. In addition to being the record of one man's life, it is a case study in the social power of an eager and original intelligence. John Cotton Dana's life is an encouragement to every individual attempting to fill his citizenship with devotion and is a glory to the profession of librarian.

The publication of this volume is a joint enterprise of the Free Public Library of Newark and the Newark Museum who have thus expressed the continuing admiration and affection which the Trustees and Staffs of these institutions hold for Mr. Dana.

In the making of this book I have had the invaluable help of Beatrice Winser and of the staffs of the Newark Public Library and the Newark Museum, among whom Marguerite Gates has been especially helpful. An especial word of thanks is due Aline Leonard who has done so much of the sifting, organizing and preparing of this material that without her help this book could not have appeared. The merits of the book must be counted as belonging to them, and if there are any errors I assume the responsibility for them.

FRANK KINGDON

TABLE OF CONTENTS

JOHN COTTON DANA

CHAPTER I

UNTO THE THIRD AND FOURTH GENERATION

THE stream of life that produced John Cotton Dana was fed at American springs. He was a product of the native soil. Every line of his ancestry runs into families that have belonged to America for more than six generations. It is impossible to capture the full flavor of his career without establishing this fact at its beginning. He was of the American earth.

When we trace the old world origins of his predecessors we find them coming from three lands—England, Scotland and France. In seventeenth century England they were united with those implacable dissenters who under Cromwell were to mobilize the elemental forces of the soil to overthrow the King, men in whom liberty was an irresistible passion until it became a tyrannical dogma. The Puritan lacked many graces but he gave the world its most impressive modern picture of the relentless power of the human will. Tensile strength was in the bone and sinew of those who inherited Puritan blood. On the Scotch side the family was associated with those who had considerable wealth and naturally, also, being Scotsmen, the desire for education. The Scot stands midway between the English and the Irish. He gives the impression of reserve, even of hardness, but underneath he is full of sentiment, mysticism, poetry and quiet humor, knowing how to laugh, but not too much. A unique combination of realism and artistry is the distinctive gift of Scotch inheritance as the hills of Scotland are full of grace but have granite at the core of them. The French strain is more difficult to trace in the Dana family but it seems well established that they belonged to the Huguenot group in which the French flair for life was combined with a depth of conviction that could withstand persecuting threats. From every side there flowed into Mr. Dana's veins the blood of those who combined pride of race with independence of judgment, and artistic joy with solidity of character.

The names belonging to his immediate American ancestry are Cotton, Dana, Loomis, Swan, Gay and Cushing. In them the ancient lines were stamped with the distinctive New England genius. They inhabited and had no small part in making that section when it dominated the cultural patterns of our developing American way of life.

The name of Cotton is probably derived from the village of that name in Kent, England. The clear line of the family may be traced to Sir Henry Cotton who lived in Cambridgeshire in the second half of the fourteenth century, being married to Anne Le Fleming in 1374. In the tenth generation from him was born the Reverend John Cotton in 1585, who came to America as a minister of the Massachusetts Bay Colony in 1633 and who died in 1652. Fifth in the line of descent from him was Mary Gay Swan who married Charles Dana and became John Cotton Dana's grandmother. The history of the Cotton family has been so thoroughly explored in writing that it seems unnecessary here to recount the contributions of its members to American history.

In France the name of Dana was spelled "Danna," but its earliest appearance in America finds it in the form familiar to us. In Cambridge, Massachusetts, the records of 1640, nine years after the founding of the town, carry the name of Richard Dana, who served his community in the varying duties of constable, surveyor of highways, tythingman and grand juror. He left seven sons and four daughters when he died about 1700 and from these a distinguished progeny has contributed many familiar names to our national story. They have shone in learning, in journalism, in medicine, in trade and finance, in literature and in every branch of the national service. Every war in which the United States has been engaged, from the colonial wars until the present, has found the name of Dana distinguished on both land and sea. Charles Dana, John Cotton Dana's grandfather, was a member of the fourth generation in descent from Richard Dana of Cambridge. It is no part of this book to explore the brilliant records of all who have borne the name of Dana, beguiling as the prospect might be to write of such men as Charles A. Dana of *The Sun* and Richard H. Dana of *Two Years Before The Mast,* or of such women as Mary Bancroft Dana [1] in whom the intrepidity of the pioneer combined with unfaltering integrity to create the very pattern of true greatness. These and others of the Dana family have become already a part of our American tradition.

The Loomis, sometimes spelled "Loomys," ancestry in America, goes back to Joseph Loomis who was born in Braintree, Essex County, England about 1590, who there followed the trade of woolen draper and who sailed from London April 11, 1638. The family settled in Windsor, Connecticut, where John, son of Joseph, was admitted to the church in 1640. He later became a deacon of the church and served as a Deputy to the General Court for fifteen years, thirteen of them consecutively. His son, Nathaniel, served as an Ensign of the Military Company in Colchester, Connecticut, being appointed October 13, 1715, and later held the same office in the Company at Bolton, Connecticut, being appointed October 11, 1722. For three years he

[1] Mary Bancroft Dana and her husband were friends of Blennerhassett. When he with Burr was accused of conspiracy a crowd of men besieged her house, believing Blennerhassett within. She barred their way with her person, defying them until her husband arrived.

also was a Deputy to the General Court, sitting from 1708 to 1710. Judge Jeduthan Loomis, John Cotton Dana's grandfather on his mother's side, was of the fourth generation from Ensign Nathaniel.

Thomas Swan, who brought this family name to America, was a physician, born in Scotland of wealthy parents and educated in England. It is said that his mother was a Stuart and that the McDonald family was close akin. He came to America in the middle of the seventeenth century and settled in Roxbury, Massachusetts. His oldest son, Thomas, also was a physician like his father. The third son of this Thomas was Ebenezer who followed the sea and died captain of a vessel at thirty years of age. Of the four sons he left, the youngest was William who grew up to be a gold- and silver-smith. He died in 1774 at the age of fifty-eight, leaving ten children of whom the seventh in age was Timothy, born in 1758. He married Mary Gay and their daughter Mary Swan was John Cotton Dana's grandmother.

The mother of Mary Gay was a great-granddaughter of the Reverend John Cotton who came to Boston in 1633. Her maiden name was Mary Cotton Cushing and she married the Reverend Ebenezer Gay who graduated from Harvard College in 1737 and built the Gay manse in Suffield, Connecticut, in 1742. The Gay family came to this country in the person of John Gay in 1630. He settled in Dedham, Massachusetts, in 1636 and it was from this home that the Reverend Ebenezer went to Suffield, where he remained as pastor for fifty-six years and was succeeded by his son. Through the Gays the Danas were descended from John Cotton, John Cushing, Sir Richard Saltonstall and George Bunker who owned Bunker Hill.[2] Among John

---

[2] As one of Mr. Dana's relatives wrote: "Whether we fought at Bunker Hill or not, we owned it."

Cotton Dana's prized possessions was a Bible bearing the name of "Mary Gay."

The mother of Mary Cotton Cushing was the grand-daughter of the senior Reverend John Cotton and the daughter of his equally well known son by the same name who was born in 1640. She married Judge John Cushing, a member of the family which came to America among the Pilgrims and which to this day has maintained itself as one of the most active and influential families in the Old Colony region of Massachusetts. It would be impossible to tell the stories of Plymouth, Scituate, Hingham, Weymouth and Braintree without constant reference to the Cushings. In "A Funeral Sermon, delivered October 25, 1796, at the interment of Mrs. Mary Gay, relict of the Reverend Doctor Gay, pastor of the first Church in Suffield, by Joseph Lathrop, D.D., Pastor of the first Church in West-Springfield" the preacher made a special point of the fact that "Mrs. Gay, whose remains now lie before us, was respectable for her parentage" being "daughter of the late Honorable Judge Cushing of Scituate."[3]

It is important to dwell thus upon Mr. Dana's ancestors because he was himself so aware of them, feeling that he was bone of their bone and flesh of their flesh. In his own files he kept a full record of their lives and their relationships. This fact, in itself, is a valuable commentary upon him. There is something of a fashion among some who would trumpet their democracy to decry an interest in family backgrounds as though it were a sort of ancestor worship smacking of aristocracy. With a greater wisdom Mr. Dana recognized that a man is defined to some degree by his inheritance, and that the pattern of his responsibility is fixed by it. He did not boast of his ancestors. He tried to live up to them. So strong, indeed, was the ancestral

[3] This sermon was published by H. and O. Farnsworth, 1797.

strain in his own personality that his biographer is tempted to pause here to demonstrate how their characteristics were combined in him. He had the strong individuality of the Cottons, the creative energy of the Danas, the civic loyalty of the Loomises, the quiet humor of the Swans and the integrity of the Cushings. From them he came and their elements so mixed in him that he was a gracious blending of them all.

Charles Dana, John's grandfather, was born in Danbury, Connecticut, in 1781. He decided to make his home in Woodstock, Vermont, where he opened a dry goods store, in partnership with General Allen, in November 1802. He married Mary Gay Swan and to them were born eight children of whom the third was a son, Charles, who was John Cotton Dana's father. The senior Dana and his wife both lived to be seventy-five years of age. There is no item of particular note to record of this man save that, as Mr. Dana once wrote, "he was quite prosperous in running a general country store." He built his home in 1807 and thirteen years later he erected his brick store on Woodstock Green in 1820. Here he continued in the business until his death in 1857. A signature of his is still extant. It is written in a large, bold Spencerian hand with elaborate and emphasized capital letters, but no flourishes. Some of the letters are not joined with their predecessors or successors and stand alone. The writing summons up the picture of a man who knew his own mind and had a clear head for business, yet one from whose temperament the finesses of sentiment were by no means absent.

Almost across the street from him lived his brother John Clark Dana who was born in 1770 and died in 1811. He practiced the trade of a cabinet maker and was known as a good workman. That this reputation was deserved may be attested by the fact that pieces of his work, the case of an old grandfather's clock and a sideboard, are said to be still in use.

Charles Dana, Jr., John's father, was born in 1813 at Woodstock in the house built in 1807 where he spent practically all his life and in which he died on July 5, 1884. Of him we know a good deal through an excellent account written at his death by Frederick Billings for the local Woodstock paper. The picture he draws is of a man faithful in all his pursuits of business and citizenship but at the same time singularly sensitive to good books. He moved among his fellow-citizens, notable for "his classic face and bearing," trusted by his neighbors in positions of public responsibility, known to have a "rare literary faculty," and mentioned as one who "would make a more successful merchant if he did not sit up so late with his books." His obituary describes him in such glowing words as these: "No man could be more faithful to his Christian vows, no one more earnest in bearing burdens, no one more loving and dutiful in seeking to keep alive the faith of the Fathers, no one more sure that the glory of the New England Village is the vigorous life of the Church of God." His life was comparatively uneventful. At sixteen he found his way to Kimball Union Academy at Meriden, New Hampshire. He returned to become his father's clerk and in 1835 became a partner in the business. He married Charitie Loomis on February 16, 1848, by whom he was the father of five sons, Charles, Harold, John Cotton, Joseph L. and Edward. For fifteen years he was a director of the Woodstock Railroad, a position to which his fellow-citizens elected him. He served ten years as a director of the Ottauquechee Savings Bank. His favorite authors were Wordsworth, Coleridge and Carlyle. Dartmouth College recognized his unusual abilities when it conferred upon him the degree of Master of Arts (*honoris causa*). Altogether, he must have been a notably perceptive and conscientious man. It certainly is not difficult to trace the profile of the father in the character of his son.

A brief glimpse of Mrs. Dana, John's mother, has been preserved for us in a letter from a John Wheeler to his daughter Lucia. He met Mrs. Dana, a childhood friend, on the cars at White River Junction. "Her husband had given me the seat by her side, as though it was a real pleasure to have his wife gratified in seeing an old friend." The conversation turned to books and he found "that her husband was a merchant, but a real Dana for books, and she evidently loved him and the child and the books." As they talked he glanced at her face and "I almost exclaimed, 'Why, who knew you had such a face?' From the lips which were ruddy and healthful—from the lips upward there was a profile of Raphael's Fornarina, as seen in the principal figure in the lower part of the *Transfiguration*. And so I looked until I began to think she would think it strange."

CHAPTER II

THE BOY

THE stuff of human life in a small town has a chance to grow into sharply etched individuality. There is enough room and freedom for the sharp corners of a personality to thrive. Where population is concentrated the rubbing of men against one another smooths off their edges and produces at least a superficial polish. In the country this does not happen and men display a more native pattern. They are their own masters. They are not caught in any hierarchy of social preferences. They live their own lives and think their own thoughts. Theirs is a prerogative of eccentricity and upon their lips is the breath of originality.

When these natural conditions work themselves out among men and women bred to pride in their independence they are emphasized in their effect. In the British Isles they produce the Scot and in the United Stated the New Englander. Of all New England Vermont is the essence. The Vermonter is as he is, and the only emotion in him that matches his independent pride is his fine scorn of those who think that because they live more easily they therefore live more wisely. He will match wits with anyone who has an egg or a horse or an idea to swap, but to all who come with any kind of missionary zeal to make him other than he is, he presents a resistant silence that approximates the tenacious glory of his granite hills.

John Cotton Dana grew up in Woodstock in the heart of Vermont. He was born there on August 19, 1856. He lived there through childhood and adolescence. Always he thought of it as home. He returned to it for his summer days in later years. And there he rests in his long sleep. Much of the great world he saw in later days and part he was of events beyond the ken of his native place, but always in his heart he was a man of Vermont. His were early days of discipline. His father was a devout man and this meant that John knew the regimen of the inflexible moral law and of the old New England Sabbath. He grew up among good books but there was no place in his home for reading that ventured into fields untrodden by the polite accepted authors. With no drama in the town his only knowledge of the stage was that gained from the efforts of the church to put on plays. One day a week he attended services with his family and learned the Scriptures and tasted sermons with a regularity as unquestioned as that he should take his best suit on that day to wear. All the authority of his beloved and dignified father was in his orthodox training and it was enough for any boy.

At home he lived with a mother to whom cleanliness was so near to godliness that sometimes the partition was too thin to notice. Neatness is no easy virtue for any boy, young or old, but the sweet tyranny of a New England mother can teach it to the most intractable, and John learned it. Years afterward he recalled how once in his childhood he was just starting off on a boyish game when he heard the undeniable voice: "You haven't finished the yard yet. Over by the store are several scraps of paper! You haven't raked the grass near the steps—it's full of dead leaves. You must rake the yard over, every bit of it!" A boy could not argue with his mother and Solomon, if a thing was worth doing, it was worth doing well. These disciplines were strict. They expressed a people of serious mind, but, contrary to some opinions, they did not make life gloomy. There was too much substance to the men and women involved. John's father was well informed and could quote his Horace as well as his Pope. Uncle Swan, his mother's brother, was a man of considerable reputation in classical learning. Many an hour John and his four brothers must have listened to good talk among the elders, mingling practical matters with that informal discussion of good books that makes them familiar friends with the warmth of the stove upon them. John was the middle boy among the five sons and this also undoubtedly supplied a measure of discipline. He could not claim the priority of the elder or seek the protection afforded the younger. He had to make his own place, and he did so vigorously. He learned in the ruthless school of his brothers how to adjust and how to protect his own identity.

Beside the wider horizons opened by books there were those revealed by his father's store. All country roads lead eventually to the local merchant's door. With just a driveway between the house and the store John grew up to the music of hoofs against the hard road, of the soft slew of the sleighs in the snow, of the whinneying of the horses and the ringing of their winter bells, and of the voices of men and women calling to each other in greeting. He learned to call people by name and to anticipate their familiar purchases. He could tell a horse at a glance and guess its weight within a few pounds. The characteristic phrases of the twanging speech of all his neighbors were as much a part of his normal world as the haze over the hill. The quiet drama of simple human events played itself out in the homespun pageantry of the goings and comings of people known.

In addition to these neighborly folk the store drew to itself consignments of goods from the ends of the earth. There were tea chests from China and Ceylon, codfish bringing the tang of the sea, sugar rich with tropical suns, and tobacco from the south. Every packing box was an emissary and a mystery coming from far places to quicken a boy's imagination and stir his curiosity. When they were emptied they became raw materials for amateur carpenters. Planing the long pine boards of which the boxes were made, John learned the pleasure of skill with a tool. He could make an article and look upon it to call it good, thus entering into the joy of the artisan, which is not far from the delight of the artist. He developed that ingenuity in making things to serve his purposes which is one of the marks of a man who has been thrown upon his own resources in the emergencies of childhood. Added to house and store there were the yard and barn. These meant chores, but also a kind of education but poorly replaced in modern manual training classes. He learned how to handle a horse, and what the feeding of a pig was like. At night he would fetch home the cows and share in milking them. Then there was the garden to plant and hoe and weed. In winter the wood was waiting for the saw and the shed had to be filled. When the snow was heavy the paths must be dug, and the back ached while the cheeks stung with sub-zero cold. Hard enough it was, but a boy grew under it, and there was leisure enough for fun.

Woodstock stands on a little stream, the Ottauqueechee. The boys could carry packing boxes to its banks and build their rafts. There was a chance to swim. The sheets of lead from the tea chests supplied admirable sinkers for the fishing lines. And sometimes it was good just to ramble along banks whose trees became one's old friends. Winter brought ice on the river for skating and while snow meant shoveling, it also meant the engaging opportunity to build snow huts, to go snow-shoeing and to enjoy sleigh-riding and tobogganning. There was ice to be cut and hauled to the ice-house, and that was as exhilarating as work could be. And sometimes on a winter day the boys went fishing through the ice.

Always there were the usual boyish games. Marbles heralded the spring in Woodstock as elsewhere. But in Vermont there is one gift of spring days that makes all other springs seem niggardly. There is new life running in the maples and that means maple syrup, cooled if you are lucky in the snow. John grew up with the bounty of syrup and sugar for a heritage.

One firm friend of the Dana boys was Charley Perry. He also was a gift of the store to them for he drove the teams and loaded the wagons or the sleds. Now Charley was a mighty man. He could lift a box of freight as other men a box of cigars. Horses obeyed his strong touch on the reins as children the guidance of a parent. Winter and summer he sat high above the freight, his shirt sleeves rolled above his elbows. The frost could not force a coat on his broad shoulders. He rode the elements and laughed at winds that pinched and painted other men's noses. He was the strong man as hero to the growing Dana lads. He approved of the boys and let them share his rides and work. From him they learned some practical mechanics. He taught them how to set the skids to slide a hogshead into the cellar, how to loop and tie the rope and how to ease the weight to a landing gentle as a paper falling. Tough as cedar was Charley and the boys adored him.

Another friend came when the wood in the yard had been cut to stove length. He was the colored man, Jim Hazard, who split it before it was carried to the shed. Jim could lay his axe to the center of a block of wood as true as Robin Hood could wing an arrow to a deer's heart. It was a feat marvelous in a boy's eyes. But Jim was more than wielder of an axe. He had tuned his tongue to California, among the men of '49, and it could spin yarns to woo the heart out of any stay-at-home. These two, Jim and Charley, were men, and wherever John went afterward he knew a man when he saw one.

The boys of Woodstock in the sixties of the nineteenth century never heard of "group work" or of "the gang instinct," but they had both and organized them into disciplined activities, as befitted men of Vermont. A little brown notebook in Mr. Dana's files contains the records of these boyish plans for clubs, each with its Constitution and By-Laws, its financial records and its motions made and carried. There was the Otta-Queechee Base Ball Club, named for the river where the raft was built, and solemnly dedicated to "the perpetuation of the American game of base-ball." Fines were imposed on the members who used profanity, resisted the lawful authority of the captain, or partook of "ardent spirits as a beverage" during meetings. This organization developed into a club that met socially all the year round, but apparently it was difficult to keep up enthusiasm during the winter, a condition aggravated by the failure of some members to bring wood for the stove when their turns came.

On September 2, 1872, the boys had a big day when they raised a flag to Grant and Wilson, candidates of the Republican Party in that presidential election year. The accounts for the occasion are complete: twine .10, hook .05, rings .07, wire .25, lettering 1.00; total 1.47. The first dollar young John earned was for a patriotic purpose. In the village was an old cannon which the boys hauled about the streets on the Fourth of July. It was "a cormorant for powder," so everybody had to contribute to a pool for the powder. John earned his contribution by gathering scraps of old iron all over the village and selling them to the junk dealer. Thus the first dollar was wearily earned and quickly spent.

The enterprise of his youthful days that most vividly caught John's imagination, however, was the publication of the little amateur sheet, *The Acorn*. It was a four page monthly and ran from May 1872 until November 1873. Its contents were largely short stories, poems, editorials, humorous anecdotes, advertisements of local firms and exhortations to the delinquent subscribers to pay their debts. The paper is neatly printed and remarkably free from typographical errors. Serious comment and good fun jostle one another in its pages to reveal the healthy adolescent minds behind it. Moreover, it gave a new breadth of outlook to these village boys for they exchanged copies with many similar publications from states as varied as California, Ohio, New York, New Jersey, Nebraska, Maryland, Massachusetts, Pennsylvania, New Hampshire, Minnesota and Virginia. The printing of *The Acorn* gave him an occupation which afforded him an opportunity to manipulate type, an activity he enjoyed down to the end. He was always skilful with his hands. One of his happiest pastimes as a boy was the making of arrows out of shingles. In these, a little ahead of the center he cut a rough notch. "These arrows," he once wrote, "would be shot by a loop at the end of a piece of elastic, which itself was tied to the end of a stick. I tell you it was grand sport."

Until he left for Dartmouth College in the autumn of 1874 John lived in Woodstock. It is an old village, the first settler arriving in 1768, and now has about 1500 population, set among the Green Mountains at the foot of Mount Tom and in the valley of the Ottauquechee River. Its streets are marked by elms and its homes have that clean contented air that speaks of the New England conscience and its careful grace. Against the surrounding hills the white spires add their slender comment of praise and prayer. Within the village John's life centered in the home and store on the Green. The river, four brothers and their mutual friends were his companions. We must not fail to repeat that these were all in Vermont, which means that over

everything was that inescapable atmosphere that lies like a
spell upon all whom it touches.

John grew up with an intimate knowledge of all that is
involved in being a part of a small community. Its limitations are well defined but within them there is the ceaseless interplay of human motives, of daily talk and familiar
activity, that mirrors the pity, cruelty and laughter that
are the elements of all men's living. A boy who has lived
his first eighteen impressionable years in a small town has
learned some facts of men and nature not found in books.
John Cotton Dana packed his bags for Dartmouth having
these lessons by heart. Before we leave for Dartmouth with
him, however, we must pause a bit to tell ourselves that
the pattern of these Woodstock days set the lines of his
development for many years. His parents had a firm authority over him which was as deeply rooted in his devotion to them as in their strength of will. He had accepted
both their rule and their doctrine, adapting himself to the
conventions of the town. Yet while he accepted the rule
of home and church he rebelled somewhat against them.
The strong strain of individualism characteristic of his race
was not content to accept things as they were without
questioning them. He was no born institutionalist. Something in him fretted against the harnesses of men.

Through college and early manhood he was continually
asserting his prerogative to be himself. He fought a long
hard fight within himself over the religious teachings of
his youth, and not for years was he to feel free of spirit. He
was enough like his father to put money in a second place
among his ambitions, but he found his meaning for experience at other altars than those of the church. Yet when
he finally found his place in the world the family pattern
lingered in his seeking his lifework within the framework
of a secure institution. The old rebellion was there also,

for he sought to make over the very institutions by which
he lived. This strain of inner conflict can be traced back
and forth through many years. It made him restless, but
the other side of restlessness is adventure. It made him
dissatisfied but dissatisfaction may prompt achievement
and in his case it did.

CHAPTER III

COLLEGE AND YOUNG MANHOOD

JOHN entered Dartmouth College in 1874. At that time the college operated on something of a part-time plan, partially resembling the alternating study and working divisions of some contemporary institutions like Antioch College. The calendar of classes was arranged to provide for the absence of students who needed to teach winter schools to earn part of their expenses. This fitted in excellently with the needs of the rural schools, for these could be handled by a woman teacher in the summer when many boys were at work, but had to have a male teacher in the winter when the big boys were present.

The college term began in the latter part of August, and there was a seven weeks vacation after New Year's followed by a seven weeks term. Then the year was completed by a term ending in July. About half the students taught during the winter weeks. School committeemen would write to the college for "the biggest man you've got," for every teacher established his authority by his physical prowess. There is no record that Mr. Dana ever had serious difficulty. He did once write, however, to his college friend, William D. Parkinson, that he would "be glad to get back where folks do not think me 'stuck up' for using a toothbrush." He received $4 a week for teaching and boarded at the home of the local committeeman.

In addition to this winter school teaching many students canvassed during the summer vacation. Mr. Dana studied and taught and sold, as did most of his friends. His brief notes and letters from his college days show him beginning to feel a drive toward economic independence. He was continually urging the necessity of finding a school at which he could teach and so earn a part of his tuition. Apparently, failing this in the first year, he tried, in good college student style, to sell subscriptions. One postcard to his father contained just the following words: "Am neither love-sick nor dead as yet, but Fish don't bite very well, times are too hard. Went to Congo Festival last evening in Church and was introduced somewhat. Canvassing is the hardest work ever I tried. Yours, John."

Another perennial experience of the college youth was his, for in the course of another message to home is this information: "At Mrs. Sanders where I'm stopping, the food is very 'high' and they evidently don't often indulge in fresh meat; but there's enough 'substance' to it to keep me moving and that's all I can ask for." He did not lose his quiet humor, however, in the midst of canvassing and uninspired meals. How well it could stand him in stead is shown by a passage from a letter written on September 12, 1875:

The mornings are getting to be rather cold nowadays, too cold in fact to study comfortably without a fire so, as we have no coal yet, we have set up a wood stove—and such a wood stove. It is an old sheet iron one which the class of '75 took to the White Mountains when camping—and as it has only three feet of pipe and no legs, we are obliged to put it on a horse about four feet tall so that the pipe will reach the chimney. The horse is one that was made to set a high plotting table on and when the stove is set on it, it brings the door about on a level with my chin. Altogether it makes the worst looking warming machine ever concocted, resembling a long necked, long legged black bodied bird more than anything else. . . . The whole thing is very simple and doesn't weigh more than twenty-five pounds, so we can waltz it into the parlor—build a fire in it and warm the room up for the day—then waltz it back into the bedroom out of the way—very handy indeed.

Accompanying this description at the point indicated by the break above was a sketch of "the warming machine" with the title below: "wery like a bird."

In February 1876 he sent an interesting self-estimate to his father, evidently in answer to a parental letter:

My "scattering" in the book line since I have come to Hanover has not been alarming by any means. So far in my course I have read hardly a dozen books, and at no time I think less than last term. But for my reading before I came much cannot be said. Possibly it was much but certainly it was scattered among many and not a very desirable many at that. I feel this now more than any one else, and while over here, with something to think of most of the time, I can generally refrain from browsing among books and instead study and ruminate a little. But my mind works slow. I have been convinced of it in the last year and a half, if never before.

In this same letter he reported that he "had to study between seven and eight, and very often nine hours a day, which, with three hours of recitation, made from ten to twelve hours of brainwork in the twenty-four." Continuing this theme in a following letter he comments: "Any let up on continual plodding breaks me up badly, and it seems sometimes as though I never should get to take any pleasure in working. I find though that if I stick and keep sticking to the business in hand, if it does not get to be pleasant, it gets to be so natural that any break is not such a source of delight." In still another letter he argues for intensive reading of few books rather than for a more discursive habit.

There are many little revelations in the preserved letters of those days that show a dutiful son with a mind beginning to assert its individual self, a painstaking student having difficulty in getting the engine of his mind spinning smoothly, and a young man putting a good face on his lack of funds, but nevertheless feeling it. "When a fellow has only a patched ten-cent scrip and a one-cent postage stamp in his pocket—he can't be very free with his letters." The pressure was relieved somewhat in his senior year for he taught in the winters of 1876 and 1877, but evidently the four years were a long, hard pull. On the academic side and in college activities he made a good record. Of the seventy-four members of the Class of 1878 he ranked fourth at graduation. Apparently he did not maintain this position consistently throughout the four years, for there is one reference in a letter to his standing eleventh in his sophomore year. The gain in position by the end of his course is another indication that his mind got into action slowly but picked up momentum as he matured. At the Class Day Exercises preceding his graduation he was accorded the honor of being one of the speakers. The subject he chose was "The Malthusian Theory of Population." He also spoke on the Commencement program, his subject being phrased in a piquant title, "The Modern Millennium, Less Work and More Pay." These orations cost him great effort apparently for he wrote his mother: "The nearer I come to it the more I am disgusted with the thought of Commencement exercises."

He was a good athlete, too, his name appearing on many of the "selected teams" of his class. In one track meet he took three firsts. It was on this occasion that he scored his most surprising triumph. One man in the college was generally conceded to be the champion at the broad jump. No one thought he could be beaten—except John Cotton Dana. He practiced steadily in the woods for weeks before the event, allowing only one faithful friend to share his secret and measure his jumps. When the day of the meet arrived, he was at his peak and beat the champion, to the amazement of the crowd. He also won the running high jump and the hurdles.

His main intellectual drive was toward philosophic subjects, but he showed intense interest in practical scientific experiments. He made the first telephone many of his classmates ever saw and, with some of his friends helping, constructed a Holtz machine, the electrical wonder of that day. This same ingenuity led him to devise novel forms of entertainment for gala days. Once, at least, he led a student protest against a faculty ruling, when the authorities declined permission to Theodore Tilton to speak in Dartmouth. During his college years he was a member of Psi Upsilon fraternity. In his junior year he edited the humorous classbook *The Aegis*. Upon graduation in 1878 he was elected to Phi Beta Kappa. His classmates generally looked upon him as the best read man of his class. He left college honored, happy and in debt.

Following college, John spent a little more than a decade filling out his personality and testing his strength and theories against various kinds of persons and interests. These thirteen years do not show much in the way of measurable achievement, but they precipitated his philosophy of life. When they were over he knew himself, had defined what he believed and had his instruments of self-expression finely turned and ready for service.

He returned to Woodstock after graduation. There he entered the law office of French and Southgate, giving himself to the study of law. He apparently stayed close to his home until the Spring of 1880. This period, in addition to his pursuit of legal training, was devoted to wide reading. It is characteristic of him that he kept a methodical list of the books read. In the little notebook containing this record are listed many volumes including works by Anthony Trollope, Tom Hood, Harriet Beecher Stowe, Henry James, T. B. Aldrich and Goethe. He also read all of Milton, Dante's *Inferno* and much of Chaucer, Shakespeare, Dryden, Wordsworth, Pope, Swift, Addison, Gray, Burns and Tennyson. In metaphysics he read Matthew Arnold, John Fiske, Tyndall, Taine and Spenser. Biography and travel rounded out his mental diet. In 1879 he wrote and printed a thirty-two page pamphlet *On Reading*. It is made up of selections from a half-dozen well-known essays on reading. He selected as he says "those parts which seem best adapted for the guidance of people in general." Thus early he gives evidence of that passion to introduce books to ordinary people which later was to dominate his career. At the end of the pamphlet he lists "The Authors To Read," naming eleven Americans, forty English, eighteen Germans, twenty-three Frenchmen, three Spaniards, six Italians, fourteen Latin authors, thirteen Greek writers and six miscellaneous including Confucius, Mencius and the Koran. These two records of books form their own comment upon the mind and interests of this boy hardly a year out of college. His own remark on this period was: "The law played second fiddle to John Fiske, German, French, the teaching of a little Latin and Greek, and reading— poetic and very miscellaneous. My thinker tries and my body makes a general kick."

In the Spring of 1880 John went out to Denver, Colorado. A classmate at Dartmouth, Frank Wadleigh Gove, had gone to Southwestern Colorado in December 1879. He became deputy United States land and mineral surveyor in the mining section of Colorado. John Cotton Dana joined him at Rico in May 1880. Probably his doubtful health prompted the move. He stayed in Colorado until the Spring of 1882. In company with Gove he worked at surveying the territory.

This was a period of rough and ready living among men unhampered by the conventional restraints of highly organized communities. Something in the young Vermonter answered to the untamed rigor of this life with its elemental friendships. He revelled in his work and enjoyed his companions. For two years he lived in tents. We have glimpses of him surveying townships in six inches of snow, eagerly awaiting the mail from home, counting himself fortunate to be able to change his underclothing once in two or three weeks, but with it all having "no definite plans for the future." Sometimes the monotony would force him to write home such words as: "I do not think you can realize the longing one has for a little something out of the ordinary line when living without change for months." He found some recreation in examining the cliff dwellings and exercised his powers of observation searching for relics of the days they represented. His thoughtful family kept him supplied with warm clothing and good shoes, thus making him the envy of his more improvident mates. Clothing, however, was not enough. He kept writing for magazines and lectures to keep his head as warm as his feet.

His letters were written on all sorts of paper. Sometimes, when far from any camp or base, he wrote in small notebooks and mailed them in envelopes. These writings are chiefly remarkable for their length. He went to great pains to describe accurately the environment in which he worked and the attendant circumstances. He was living outdoors, walking long distances, getting a taste of frostbitten feet, stumbling on old ruins and, occasionally, cocking his gun at the rumors of Indians or bears prowling about. His own state of mind can be seen in the following sentences from a letter home: "From my environment one would not judge me to be advancing in the legal profession. I am engaged in that occupation about which the books throw such a halo of fun and excitement—'Roughing It.' Still my experience is, and will be, valuable to me—and give me the shekels, so I am at present satisfied!"

The two years, 1880–1881, served to give him an experience wholly different from that of Woodstock and Dartmouth. He tasted a country of no boundaries. He lived where tradition played a minor part. He wandered over open spaces and into half-made towns. He saw human societies before they had crystallized. His mind saw life in new dimensions and was emancipated from the limitations of provincial conventions. His letters are full of his observations of the terrain and the community. He illustrates them with rough sketches of the hills and the courses of the streams. There are occasional glimpses of the people: "The Navajo squaws make the blankets with the rudest kind of looms, spinning and dyeing most of the wool. For some colors they unravel the government blankets which they buy of the Utes. The Navajos are self-supporting." Meanwhile there are glimpses of himself: "I must record my triumph of making four mince and one apple pie this afternoon, which are pronounced very good. The undercrust does *not* stick to the teeth." And again: "I have to shake the snow off the bed every night and often in the morning. . . . Mostly I sleep comfortably—and am sure of enough fresh air!" He sent a long and enthusiastic letter about his visit to the Calumet and Hecla mine. Running through his correspondence is continual comment on books. He mentions incidentally having Sartor Resartus in his pocket at one time. At another he writes of his annoyance when men with fifteen- or twenty-cent cigars ask him for "something to read": "The idea is that tobacco is a necessity and a book a luxury."

Long journeys through the hills surveying the country brought accounts that must have amazed and sometimes almost dismayed the gentle folks back home. There were weeks when he was without any meat save bacon. The undisciplined men of the country ran wild with their guns and once killed a man with whom Dana had been friendly and whose house he had used as a base of supplies. One day he came upon a lone prospector tapping away at a rock in the hope of striking a stake. Water had to be taken as it was found and much of it was strong with alkali. He was often twenty or thirty miles from a post-office and would get his letters from home in packages of three or four. Apparently he observed but did not share the wilder life of the men about him. To his mother he writes: "I have been thinking lately of how great a help it has been to me in my trying to live as one should, since I have been out here, that I had such a mother and father. I am away from religious influences for months at a time, but that does not prevent my knowing and feeling what is right living, and I owe the knowledge to those at home." These were the last words he wrote to her.

The closing days of August 1881 were heavy with the realization of his mother's failing health and on September 1 he learned of her death. His letters reveal his devotion to her. On August 21 he wrote his father:

Mother's failing is the saddest of news to me and it is something about which I cannot write. All summer long as I have thought of her I have wished I might be at home, though I have not known that I could be of use and have felt that mother was having the best of care. And now I cannot help thinking that you would not hesitate to send for me could I give mother any pleasure by coming or could I be of any service.

He telegraphed his inability to get home after the final news came and on September 3 he sent his letter:

I cannot make it seem true—the house without mother—although my letters have been preparing me for it for so long. . . . But that she is gone, I can't realize it. I can hardly help reproaching myself that I was not there yet I felt that you at home know best what I should do. . . . I know how the home must seem broken up to you but please don't say it is altogether so. A homecoming cannot be what it was, but I don't want to think that there is no such thing. . . . I am glad you wrote me the long letter you did. It told me just what I was most anxious to know. I can write no more of it now.

The end of 1881 saw him back in Denver and Colorado Springs. His mind was playing with the idea of deserting the law and of turning to some other means of livelihood. It was characteristic that he should turn to books: "My thoughts have turned often to the idea of taking up some business instead of the law. . . . Some kind of manufacturing or book publishing are what I have in mind. The difficulty is to find a place where one can advance as he learns. . . . What would you think of the plan?" His letters are full of enquiries for his father's advice on settling his profession: "What would you say to my going into a law office in Denver and working into a practice? I wish you would give me your opinion and tell me what you would like me to do." Two years of footloose wandering had left him anxious to settle down.

During these years, however, an important experience of another kind had come to him. Some letters to *The Woodstock Standard* had appeared in print. Thus the author in Dana began to bud. It must have made some of his old neighbors rub their eyes to read his accounts of his camping clothes and habits, but the letters are written so directly and so patently without ostentation that there can be no doubt of their gaining an audience. Their style is almost conversational. For instance, he introduces his description of himself and his traveling companions on the trail with: "I wish I could come into town some afternoon with my outfit and make a camp in the Park. It would be second only to a circus." Probably the first letters printed were ones sent to his father and seized upon by the editor. But here, at any rate, was the luxury of authorship, his own words on the printed page.

He left Colorado in the early Spring of 1882. Before bidding the State goodbye, however, he wrote an article for a Denver paper in which he scored the chilling social atmosphere of Colorado Springs. He was evidently a bit tired of the West and anxious once more to see the East and his friends. His letters are unusually sharp in their expressions. Advocating a classical education, he writes: "The average graduate of a technical school is a conceited ass." Again he says: "A conceited westerner is the most disagreeable of mortals." These comments are not unnatural. He was one by this time in whom the East and West had met. The provincialism of either was bound to stir his disapproval. Henceforth, he was emancipated from the narrower conventions of the East, but he never lost his understanding of its inner qualities of strength. The winds of the West had blown through his mind. He had seen human beings in pioneer conditions and everything thereafter he measured by elemental human standards. But his heart never left Vermont. The West liberalized him but his foundations were in the granite. He had left the East a boy seeking health and adventure, he came back to it a man in the process of establishing his own individual philosophy of life. The scion of the Danas and the Cottons had tramped and camped beyond the Mississippi.

CHAPTER IV

SETTLING DOWN

IN April 1882 John returned to the East, visiting relatives and friends in Winona, Minnesota, Chicago and Cleveland on the way. After a brief visit to his home in Woodstock he went to New York where he obtained a clerkship in the law office of Bristow, Peet and Opdyke at 20 Nassau Street. His oldest brother, Charles, was now a doctor practicing in New York and his home became the center of John's activities. Friends and acquaintances from Vermont and Dartmouth provided a social circle and the young man entered fully into the life of the city with all the zest of one who had been away from metropolitan centers for two years. His letters are full of theaters, operas, books and churches. Of one service he writes: "Heard Dr. Bevan at the Brick Church this morning. He preached well, and in a way apologized for leaving his country. I am inclined to think that while he is sincere enough in his ideas he lacks a certain suavity—and has never forgotten he is an Englishman."

Behind these cultural pursuits, however, there was always his work and the continued pressure for money, in spite of what he had earned and saved in the West. His uncle Swan was rather critical of the way he spent his funds. In reply, John pointed out that he had been two years away and so needed to replenish his wardrobe, and sent on for the family inspection a statement in detail of his expenses for fourteen weeks which totalled $285. Apparently this accounting satisfied the thrifty elders back home. As for his work in the office, a characteristic comment is: "Have been through the week and by making constant mistakes am able to learn a little something." In October the need for money forced him to take a position as tutor to a family of Duryeas, teaching two boys and two girls between the ages of eight and thirteen, four hours a day, five days a week at a dollar an hour. "My pupils are pleasant and bright," he says, "and I find the work not very tedious." In fact he finds his own mind quite "elastic" after four hours of teaching. This teaching position he kept until he left New York, spending part of the summer with the Duryea family at Hempstead, Long Island. The relationship seemed thoroughly congenial although it presented the periodic pains that all teaching involves: "The pupils get on well and I take kindly to them. My great trial is the girl of ten who cannot reason when the process involves more than two ideas. '6 apples for 12¢, how many for 24¢?' is beyond her analysis. But I have hopes." A modern enough note crops out on another occasion: "The children get on though I am at sea as to 'methods' every now and then. You can imagine that my methods of teaching drawing, for instance, must be unique."

Studying law and tutoring did not exhaust his time. There is a glimpse of him at a reception "bobbing about in a swallow tail in a very acceptable way." He heard Patti in "La Traviata" and mentions attending performances of "Carmen" and "Aida." He saw Joseph Jefferson as Rip Van Winkle, attended *The Rivals*, and thought Lily Langtry a failure as Rosalind in *As You Like It*. The theater fascinated him and so when his brother Joseph visited him in New York he could not pass over Joe's failure to respond, although he excuses him on grounds of family reticence: "Joe is enjoying his visit though like the rest of the Danas he enthuses very little." He advised this younger brother to let himself go a bit: "Joe labors under the same difficulty that most of us boys do—that is reticence. I urged him to cultivate his tongue and even talk against time when opportunity offered." We can hear the talk of the two brothers walking home through the gas-lit New York streets after the show was over.

Always there were books to read and to discuss. "It is perhaps because I am at a critical stage in my experience that I have a poor opinion of the novels and essays our own writers are giving us. However it is, they seem to have no starch. Powerful clever many of them, and titillate our intellects pleasantly in the reading, but like cookies, they are nothing when they're eaten." He could pick a good book when it appeared, however. "I waste too much time on magazines, papers and the 'last novel' as I always have —and the last novel continues pretty poor picking. Have you tried to read any of the story called *Lorna Doone*? It would be worth your while to turn it over for the sake of the style and some of the descriptions. A possible recommendation of it is that it fell dead from the press and had to be pushed into notice. Now it has been through twenty various editions from ten cents to as many dollars." An illuminating sidelight on the literary stimulus that came to him from within his family comes out of a letter telling his father of a visit to the Astor Library to examine translations of the *Odyssey*. After detailing his own searches he adds: "Can you tell me if Uncle Swan admires any one translation above all others?" There is an echo of old talks about books in a question like that. In another place he writes again to his father: "I don't find that books fail me at all. Indeed as you know they are one of the things that do stay by." Books were standard currency in the Dana family.

John's work in the law office went on steadily as he devoted himself to mastering his profession. Occasionally New York seemed discouraging. He complains of dyspepsia and of special favors given to clerks from wealthy families that are on friendly terms with the partners. "Dollars go," he complains, "where dollars are and the rich have friends among the rich." On May 26, 1883, he took his written examination for the Bar. He passed so excellently that he was excused from the oral test. When the announcement of his passing was made he celebrated by buying himself a copy of Oliver Wendell Holmes' *Common Law*. On June first he was sworn in and became officially a member of the New York Bar.

One comment on New York as it was is interesting: "One apartment house I pass every day at the corner of 38th Street and Madison Avenue is eleven or twelve stories high and impresses me with its immensity. Think of an earthquake here some day!" Another feature of New York life that is not so outdated called for this comment: "Mrs. H. doesn't occupy herself enough, I think. And that is the basis of a good many of the 'feeble women' in a city. Their world is too small though they think themselves in the middle of the universe." With his Bar examination out of the way he had difficulty locating a position. "I have been a good deal discouraged at the outlook. The conclusion seems to grow on me that I was never born to 'get on.' I seem to lack the knack of 'rushing around' that some men have, or seem to have, tho' if work lies at my hand I can generally do it. Well, we'll see." Meanwhile his friends were inviting him to various ventures. He seriously considered joining one of them, Warren Fields, in a cattle- and sheep-raising ranch in Montana. It remained, however, for his old college friend, Parkinson, to persuade him to leave New York. In March 1894 John made a visit to Woodstock to see his father and then left for Fergus Falls, Minnesota, where Parkinson lived.

When he arrived at his destination he found a city of five thousand population boasting twenty-four lawyers of whom twenty were practicing. No wonder that he wrote home, "The chance for the new lawyer is slim." He started out immediately, however, to find a suitable town in which to locate. He settled on Ashby, Minnesota, though not without some doubts: "Could I go there and keep my life or ambition? Would I stagnate? Would the four or five years spent in so small a place be of any benefit to me in the long run? Supposing I got on well, would my success be as good a thing really as several years of gravel scratching among real men?" It was about this time that his brother, Dr. Charles, wrote a sharp letter criticizing John for not settling down definitely somewhere to do something. John accepted the criticism as not unjustified but maintained his own course. He hung out his shingle in Ashby, then a shipping point and supply station for the farmers surrounding it. His home and office were in a comfortable downstairs room at the hotel and soon he had enough business to see a month or two ahead. In the same month that he moved to Ashby an article from his pen appeared in the *Albany Law Journal* (May 29, 1884) on "Responsibility—With a Forecast." It is a discussion of insanity offered as a defense in criminal action. He bases his discussion on definitions and explanations of (i) the legal meaning of responsibility, and (ii) the states of mind which the law regards as relieving from responsibility. His forecast is of the legal clarification of what responsibility really is.

Hardly was he well established in Ashby when disturbing news came from home. His father began to fail in health. "Strange that so soon after my leaving," he writes to his brother Harold, "Father should begin to fail so rapidly. Just as Mother did four years ago. Does Father say anything about seeing me?" On July 5 he received word of his father's death. This touched him more deeply perhaps than any event of his experience hitherto. His father had been his teacher, his counselor and the one to whom through all the years he had poured out his thoughts and his confidences. He had shared with him his enthusiasms, his humor and his plans. He had relied on him for decisions and for care. In John's life nobody had loomed as large as his father. With the passing of this man, whom in so many ways he resembled and whose habits of thought were so congenial, John stood alone as he had never before stood. In later years he used to say that he did not grow up as young as most boys. The truth behind this saying is probably that he carried a sense of dependence upon his father until the latter's death. This event threw him entirely upon his own judgment and so developed a new kind of independence in him.

A week after his short note acknowledging the news of his father's passing, he wrote a longer letter to his brother Harold in which he said: "I think all your and Charley's letters have come to hand. It was good to get them of course, and yet it seemed as if each one was harder to read, for as the days went by I realized more and more what had happened at home. It seems more impossible that I should not sit down and write to father the Sunday letter I have been in the habit of sending him for so many years. We boys must be all the more to each other now, if that is possible. I hope you will write me often. You can hardly realize what an affection I have for Woodstock and the home, in spite of the changes."

His work as a lawyer did not consume all his energies at Ashby. The printing press, that old love of his, recalled him. He became editor of the local paper, *The Ashby Avalanche*. His comment on its news values was: "Little happens of course to chronicle. You can tell that by the columns of the *Avalanche*. See how you like the taffy I give the Norwegians and Ashby generally." Though he poked fun at himself and his paper he really enjoyed it. A stick of type was always an adventure for him. The returns for his journalism gave him the necessities of life. "I am getting up the copy and reading proof for the paper and for that I have my board ($15 a week), office rent ($1.25) and a pass between here and Fergus when I want it, and perhaps to St. Paul should I need or care to go." He considered the possibility of buying the paper but abandoned the idea. Some of his neighbors wanted him to run for County Attorney. He played with the idea but finally declined. The truth of the matter was that his eyes were turning back to Colorado. His cousin, Edward Sabin, was a real estate operator in Colorado Springs and he invited John to join him. This suggestion stirred John's memories of Colorado and Ashby suffered by contrast: "Even two or three years of my life here in this dreary, malicious, Norwegian, *cold* place is sometimes too much for my courage." His emphasis on "*cold*" explains his aversion. At any rate, after one summer in Ashby he went West again in September. During the winter he worked with his cousin at real estate and insurance in Colorado Springs.

In the Spring of 1885, when John was twenty-nine years old, he joined a surveying party employed by the Colorado Midland Railroad to test the possibility of a branch-line from Leadville to a neighboring coal field. This survey was soon abandoned, however, and he transferred to a construction party on the road's main line. During this period he formed a friendship with Aaron M. Burt, a man some eleven years his junior. As he remarks in a character sketch he wrote some years later: "I found myself at once attracted to him and soon formed with him the friendship that grew closer, warmer and more intimate up to the very day of his death." "Shorty" Burt was his companion in long walks over the mountains and a continual joy to his friend because of a certain puckish quality that could touch all occasions with humor and turn disappointment into jest. "We told each other," Dana writes, "how the world was getting on, how we could improve it, but never how we could prevent its being an entertaining and fairly humorous place."

An article which appeared in *The Chicago Current* dated June 27, 1885, shows John wrestling again with the subject of the responsibility of individuals for their actions, but not this time as in the *Albany Law Review* from a legal standpoint so much as from a more fundamental ethical one. He called his composition "Progress and Woman" but his interest is deeper than the title indicates. He attempts to state the limits of voluntary action and to indicate the inevitability of humans behaving just as they do in certain situations. Where behavior is inevitable it is predictable and upon predictability a genuine science of social understanding can be built. "The conception of sin as the manifestation of uncaused, wilful human depravity is only the most striking example of a view of the universe in which causation is not a necessary element. Until that view is abandoned the treatment of social problems must be a continued series of experiments, ending in failure." From this premise of causation as a social factor he passes on to his consideration of woman's part in the world. "The world, the universe, being what it was, woman became what she did become as inevitably as the grain of wheat develops in the ear." He then proceeds to plead for the improvement of opportunities for women in their physical, intellectual, social, political and moral lives because added opportunity will provide fuller development. The whole article is a vigorous argument for intelligent and planned improvement of the quality of human living.

Meanwhile his pen was experimenting with verse and
The Journal of Education published these lines:

A Thought from Pike's Peak

Though at thy foot we dwell, though we believe
By daily sight 'tis given to apprehend
Thy grandeur, though thy heights we dare ascend

We know thee not; full knowledge we ne'er gain
Of thee, nor learn how all o'ertopped by thee
Thy rivals are, until from far we see
Thy peak rise lone and grand above the plain.

Thus lofty souls, the while on earth they dwell
Though honored much, though we may deem we know
Their worth, and all their greatness see full well:

We know them not; 'mid men we purblind go,
And only then the truly great can tell
When out wide plains of years afar they show.

Abstract problems did not absorb all his mind. He was
intensely interested in his neighbors and attempted to in-
terpret them to the people back home. *The Vermont Standard*
printed a letter of his "Mormons at Work" in which he
pleads for a pragmatic and fair judgment of the Mormons
as opposed to vicious tirades against their orthodoxy. He
does not argue for their ideas. He is content to tell the
story of their industriousness and plain living. This he does
with an eye-witness account of men and women whom he
sees every day. He recognizes that his data may not be
complete enough for a comprehensive judgment but he
submits his own observations as evidence to be taken into

account. "It is perhaps impossible to judge of all Mormons by these samples, even though they come from a typical Mormon settlement. But certainly their pleasant ways, their industrious habits, their cheerfulness, their comparative freedom from the exceeding vulgarity of graders, not to say of the average working man everywhere—all these speak loudly in favor of the Mormon."

A week after this letter appeared in the *Standard* there was another one filled with a lively description of the city of Leadville. In 1886 its wilder days were over but it was still a place of violent and blatant masculinity. Tom Hyman ran one of the leading dens of the place and he flaunted his defiance of all pious conventions by hanging an ironic sign over his bar, "Please do not swear," and by having a huge pulpit Bible riveted to an oak stand in front of the bar. Another hostelry boasted the sign "Russell House, by God." Dana had the feeling apparently that much of this vulgarity was a pose: "Rocky Mountain towns have a reputation for badness to maintain, and it sometimes seems that the residents feel the responsibility." For one month at this period Dana preached in a Unitarian pulpit in Boulder. This activity was not congenial and, besides, as he himself has said, "I was working a very different lead from Unitarianism."

His work for the Colorado Midland Railroad brought him in the early months of 1887 to the booming town of Glenwood Springs. Here he helped to lay out the railroad yard and worked on the grade. He was superintendent of construction of the First National Bank Building of that day, having a negro crew under him. And here he purchased a half ownership in a little house at the end of a road at the foot of the mountains. During this period he met Adine Rowena Waggener at the home of her brother-in-law who was one of the surveyors with whom Dana worked. The story goes that she heard Dana talking to someone in another room and immediately said, "Where is the man with that voice?" She found him and on November 15, 1888, they were married, with Frank Gove and his wife as the witnesses. Mrs. Dana was four years John's junior. She was born in 1860 in Russelville, Kentucky. During the years immediately preceding her wedding she had lived in Austin, Texas. Her tastes were apparently musical for within a month of the wedding she invested $425 in a piano.

John had taken up a ranch three miles from Glenwood and there he and his wife made their first home together. It was during this period, culminating in the winter of 1888–89 that he passed through the final stages of a long intellectual struggle with the orthodox religious tenets of his early training. Although his mental suffering had been intense in this experience, and it had carried on through eight years, he came out of it serene in his own mind and without bitterness toward the past. His emancipation from old dogmas broke into print in two vigorous letters on religion to the *Rocky Mountain News*: "For myself I say to the clergy . . . 'If this you tell me is not your last, best and truest thought—not another syllable to me!' I want no fairy tales, no false symbols in my religion. I am hearty enough to feed on the strong meat of truth." He urged less emphasis upon the idea of the depravity of man, a more thorough examination of the actual sources of morality and a sanely critical approach to the Bible. Not only with his pen but with his voice he emphasized his convictions. At Glenwood Springs he delivered a series of lectures on these subjects to "a large audience which included many of the most intelligent ladies and gentlemen in the city." A reporter of these occasions remarks: "The young lecturer possesses much of originality and is earnest in his

delivery." At the end of the account of one lecture, however, is the ominous forecast, "He will probably be straight-
ened out from the different pulpits in the city to-day."
If these lectures served no other good purpose they crystallized his own thinking and forced him to be ready to
defend his positions. At this time also he gave a lecture
explaining and supporting Henry George's Single Tax
Theory. In his own words he "passed through a mild attack of socialism," as an eager mind like his was almost
bound to do.

More important than any of these excursions, however,
was one into the function of the public school. On February
16, 1889 an article on "The Public School" appeared in
the *Denver Arbitrator*. The burden of its analysis is that while
Denver's school system stands well among other systems
in the United States, the whole public school system fails
to educate: "Is the average child trained for the average
life? The average boy has hands; can he use them? And
eyes; can he see with them? Our children know of Lake
Titicaca and Timbuctoo; but have they heard of the water
question which awaits Colorado's solution? They have news
of Chaucer, Jupiter, the mountains of the moon and the
Three Graces; but do they know a decent from an indecent
newspaper, or fresh air from foul? Is it not a fact, too notorious, that the boy discharged from our schools . . . finds
himself burdened with information which he does not need,
needing the knowledge which he has not, ignorant of the
sentiments which rule the world and weak in his power of
observing, of thinking, and of doing?

"If public school education be compulsory, or if the tax-
ation which supports it be compulsory, and it is adminis-
tered by the government, by the state, the state will give
no higher, no better, no more complete education than it
can itself see the utility of. Education, then, will always be,

not the product of the best thought of the best minds, but the product of the average thought of the average minds.

"The public school must be mechanical. That it may 'work' it must drive its pupils, each and all, around the same little circle of its stated curriculum, and it must strive to cast them all in the same mold. But, 'the essence of barbarism is equality.' The shadow of death upon a nation is a growing likeness in its units. However elaborate, then, be the furnishings of the public school, in so far as it works toward making our children of one mind, it works against civilization.

"Where shall we turn for relief in this matter? . . . Who can tell? To abolish the system, is past hope. In time, we may believe, it will fall by its own weight. In the schools sustained by private means there is, perhaps, a promise and a desire, in religious or sectarian schools a very dim, prophecy of the education of the future. But long before any true education shall be the common birthright of our children, it must cease to be said of us that 'we pay best: first, those who destroy us—generals; second, those who cheat us—politicians and quacks; third, those who amuse us—actors and singers. And last of all, those who instruct us.' "

This letter apparently attracted attention for in May of 1889 when the school board of Denver established the public library of that city Dana became its first librarian. In addition he was secretary to the board of education. This was his thirty-third year and he had come into his own.

CHAPTER V

THE EXPERIMENTING LIBRARIAN

THE Denver Public Library began in 1889 as a library opened by School District Number One in the belief that it would supplement the work of the schools. The school law of Colorado permitted the establishment of a public library by any school district in the State. For the purchase of books for such a library a tax of one-tenth of a mill could be levied on the property of the district. The library's other expenses might, by implication, be met by appropriations by the school board from the regular school fund. They were thus met in this district. Arapahoe County, Colorado, was divided into several districts for school support and administration. District Number One included, in 1889, forty-three per cent of all the people in the county. It enrolled 13,000 pupils in the schools. In this district Mr. Dana became Secretary of the Board of Education and first librarian of its library.

In the years immediately preceding his appointment Dana had passed through a period of hard thinking that had brought him to a restatement of his intellectual premises in his own terms. He had finally thrown off his earlier convictions which had been largely those he had accepted on the authority of his parents and teachers and had won his way through to positions of his own. He now faced a world with which he had come to terms in his own head. The struggle had been fierce but he came out of it with a feeling of exhilaration. He was sure of himself and of his own powers and he rejoiced in the free play of an emancipated mind. This was to be his chief pleasure throughout the rest of his days. He had set down his own account of

his achieved intellectual positions and he was always ready
to tilt a lance for them:

I am an agnostic religiously. I labored with the hosts of orthodoxy
for some eight years, finally conquered, and in my present freedom
can think without much bitterness of the religious atmosphere of
New England in general and Dartmouth College in particular . . .
this, although I sometimes feel as if much of the years of struggle
to escape from it were worse than wasted.

Since about 1887 I have gained a much clearer view of the great
truths, and am pleased to announce myself an egoist, a pessimist
and an anarchist. I am proud to state that during the revival of
long range philanthropy I was able to found the Society of Friends
of Human Freedom.

I passed through a mild attack of socialism, and subscribe to the
Henry George theory in a measure. I am a thorough-going free
trader and an unterrified Jeffersonian Democrat.

He immediately applied this same intellectual vigor to
the organization of the Denver Public Library and to the
work of acquainting the city with its resources. He advertised the library extensively. When word of this reached
the ears of other librarians he at once became a storm
center within the profession. Such an unorthodox and un-
dignified procedure outraged all the traditions of a profession that had gone its quiet and dusty way providing
collections of books for book lovers and letting them come
when they chose to get them. It was an unheard-of thing
for a librarian to cry his wares in the ears of the passers-by
in an attempt to make books a part of the lives of common
men. The more conservative of his fellows called him a
radical and saw him laying vulgar hands upon ancient
practices in their field. Dana went his own aggressive way.
A library was to be used. The more people who used it the
better public library it was. His work was to get the people
to read the books and to get the books the people would

read. With this as his aim he set himself to bring the men and women off the street into his institution and to send them back across its threshold with books in their hands. He wanted to take the library out of the cloister and put it on the sidewalk. Traditionalists might rage and institutionalists imagine a vain thing, but he set his course and he followed it.

He succeeded. In 1890 his library lent for home use 1,709 books; in 1891, 5,423, and in 1892, 7,486. In 1890 there were 1,470 names registered; in 1891, 4,145, and in 1892, 7,967. He awakened Denver to the fact that it had a library. His success awakened the whole library profession to the fact that it had a wide constituency to serve of which it had been largely unaware. His experiments in his first years as a librarian began a revolution throughout the entire field of library practices. His independence of judgment and action, moreover, did not wean him away from co-operation with the American Library Association. He supported its establishment of standards and endorsed its *Journal*. In the issue of November 1890 there is a note from him which says: "My only criticism of the *Library Journal* and of the reports of the conventions is that they aggravate the feelings of the librarian who wants to do the many good things suggested, and has not time, ability, money or books to accomplish them. They are utterly destructive of anything like self-satisfaction."

As part of his program of arousing interest in reading and also as an expression of his perennial love of writing and publishing, he put out a monthly magazine at one dollar a year which he called *Books*, and which had a circulation of 5000 copies. It contained quotations from all kinds of literary sources, many articles on reading and writing, and his own observations. These latter reveal him most often in the role of gadfly. He loved to puncture pretense, particularly of the pedagogical kind and to prick the mind awake with provocative assertions. "The old books superior!" he cries. "It would be easy to select from the writings of the past twenty-five years a body of literature, in the proper sense of that word, which the world can far less afford to lose than all that was written previous to that time." In another place he protests against a pursuit of the reading of history as though some special virtue of learning were in it. "The rank and file of history readers . . . get certain polite learning. But if they wish to broaden their minds, to enlarge their sympathies, to correct their views of life, to profit by the experience of their fellows, they will read, before the dry-as-dust history, the great novels of the world's great artists. Into histories have gone plodding patience and tireless research; into novels have gone these— and genius."

An interesting fragment of correspondence between John and his brother Charles published in 1892 reveals that the former had not only settled in his profession but also had fixed his own definition of success. He discards the making of money, represented in these letters by the accumulation of $100,000 at the age of forty, as a proper aim, and substitutes therefor "the spread of ideas," by which he meant inoculating more of the coming generation with the principles and doctrines of modern thought. As he himself says, this may sound " 'hifalutin' certainly; but only on six days of the week—on the seventh it is the divine message." Human or divine, it became the star by which he steered his course. In spite of his discarding money as a measure of success he did not hesitate to plunge into the debate on bimetallism which stirred Colorado and its neighboring states during the wave of Populism in the nineties. On December 3, 1893, he spoke to the Sunday Club on "Money." His thesis was that the difficulty with silver interest was "not a monopoly of legal tenders, not the gold basis, but the difficulty is with the general basis, the basis of intelligence." His proposal was that as long as there is property in land and the passing of ownership in the land from hand to hand, there is real value in the land itself, and that this constitutes a sufficient basis for the issuance of notes and bills of trading which, in their own right, can operate independently of money, whether in coins or bills. It was an attempt on his part to apply the teaching of Henry George to this specific debate. In spite of the fact that he tried to disarm criticism by asserting that he knew nothing about money he was questioned vigorously in the ensuing debate. Apparently he did not convince his hearers, but he closed the discussion by saying that he was trying, as one would guide a small boy lost in the woods, to start them a little bit on the way home.

With all his own intellectual alertness, he continually insisted on the right of people to take their lives and their books at their own level. "Better a shallow mind than an empty one. It is a proper function of a public library to amuse." Nevertheless, "With a little—or much, if necessary—judicious advertising, and with a change from the sacred trust to the utility idea of the public's collection of books, there is not a library in the country that might not be pushed to the limits of all its resources, though it had on its shelves not a book not approved by men of sense, brains and reading."

He gave encouragement to what he called "The Literature of Business" and put a mercantile library into the Chamber of Commerce Building. His voice sounded with no uncertain note on the meaning he attached to what he was doing: "Browning and Dante, and the gossip of dead royalty are well enough in their way and at their proper time and place; but a wide diffusion of knowledge and common sense about business, money, credit, transportation and trade, would do more than anything else to set the world on the high road to that general diffusion of well-to-do-ness which is the first essential of all progress." His using of the resources of the Public Library to serve the business man and the student of business opened a whole new field to library work, and gained it valuable allies in influential quarters. It was a distinct step toward identification of the library with the life of the community as it was actually lived.

Alongside it, we must place the establishment of a children's room. The first children's room, properly so called, to be established in this country was that in the Denver Public Library in September 1894.[1] It opened with about 3000 volumes for young people. On a wall above the cases were printed in large letters Stevenson's lines, "The world is so full of a number of things, I'm sure we should all be as happy as kings." There were several low tables. The upper parts of the bookcases were reserved for pictures and bulletins. On the tops of the cases were casts, vases, etc. In fact in this room at that time were nearly every one of the features of children's rooms that in later years came to be considered as important. The room was supplied with a special attendant part of the time. Children were allowed free access and were given only such supervision as was needed. *The Outlook* carried his own description of the Children's Room in its issue of September 26, 1896. This room was more than a pleasant kind of bookish nursery. It was one expression of a conviction that played a large part in directing all of Dana's activities, namely, that people should be allowed to blaze their own trails in the world of ideas and the kingdom of books. He expressed this with great clarity in an address which he delivered at the Amer-

[1] John Parsons, "First Children's Room," *Library Journal*, December 1909.

ican Library Association's Conference at Lake Placid in 1894, in the course of a discussion of university extension:

Some one asks why people object to university extension. I do not like the term, or the thing itself, for several reasons. . . . The university extension scheme is in direct opposition to the spirit of a remark that a friend of mine is fond of making, to the effect that we shall not have true education in this or any other country until we have eliminated the teacher. . . . We are in danger of being overtaught. We are always in danger of submitting too much to authority. There is a growing tendency in this country, as in others, to unify all systems of education; so far to unify them that the child shall be, from the beginning to the very end of his school life . . . in the hands of people of one mind and one thought as regards what constitutes education, and what are the proper and axiomatic views on all questions.

If this university extension work can be kept, in the main, apart from the universities, and be of the kind . . . in which men sit down and discuss things frankly and freely, with no thought of subjection to text-books, teachers, university degrees, or accepted canons, each one putting forth heartily his own ideas, it would be difficult to offer any objection to it. But for a man from an old established university . . . to go from one community to another, and attempt to fasten onto those communities the ideas dominant in that university, is to some extent an injurious thing. . . . The university has enough to do at home, and though it stay at home its influence will be as potent as, if we are wise, we shall permit it to be.

Later at that same conference he participated in the discussions to reveal that he was willing to follow the logic of his position to its conclusion:

. . . The president in his address . . . alludes to the social unrest, and to the wild and ignorant theories, and to the strikes and disturbances of one kind and another, that are continually taking place in this country, as themselves ills, and as omens of greater ills. It takes, however, only half a thought to gather from these things comfort and consolation. May we not believe that the fact that the people are in a state of unrest is a good thing rather than a bad

one? It assures us to a degree, of the continuance of the progress
we think we have been making in the last 200 years.

Toward this belief in new doctrines, . . . toward all these factors
in the general unrest, the public library happily does its part. . . .
It is not an institution in which accepted canons alone are taught.
. . . It is the extension to the humblest of the chance of learning
the latest thing that is being taught and being said. The average
man will go wrong at first, no doubt. But . . . wrong views are the
steps to the right views. No views are not even the beginnings of
wisdom. So, the public library is, above all things, educating the
individual, educating for personality, educating for the one thing
that it seems to me is to be desired, and is above all others essential
for the continued progress of the human race, that there shall be a
multitude of differing opinions.

From this point of view . . . it is not altogether correct to consider that the public library is primarily a great engine for creating
good citizens. It is primarily a great engine for creating good individuals. Let us bear in mind the remark that a good man will
not obey the laws too well. We should rejoice that we have in our
hands an instrument by means of which we may create, perhaps
not the man who fits exactly into the social order to-day, but
possibly here and there the man who does not fit into the social
order to-day but may, none the less, prove to be the man who will
give the world a fillip on its way.

This emphasis upon the free play of individuality was
no mere statement of an ideal, but was the working principle on which he organized the library itself. From the
very start he adhered to the "doctrine that the people who
establish and maintain a library are the people who own
it, and that for them alone it should be managed." He gave
the patrons of his institution every freedom possible. Reference books, reference files of magazines and all other books
were open to the public's hands. In 1896 he reported: "The
universal opinion of patrons of the library is that its open
shelf method of administration needs only to be experienced
to be approved." Here was no conventional attribution of

virtue to his own administration for later in the report he declared: "For more than a year it has frequently happened on the afternoons of winter days and especially on Sundays that the seating capacity of the library has been overcrowded; and the quarters are too narrow for good work at all times." Such a condition continued even though he put stools for readers in place of chairs and eliminated, or made less accessible, newspapers and popular periodials. The simple fact was that his fellow-citizens had caught the contagion of his own enthusiasm as it was expressed in this paragraph:

The library should be the most inviting, the most wholesome, the most elevating and the most popular place in the city for those who, without comfortable homes, wish to while away an hour or two. It should attract such visitors and it should hold them. This applies especially to young people.

He was always trying to catch his readers young. In addition to the establishment of the first Children's Room, it was also he who inaugurated the practice of lending teachers from one to fifty books for use in the school room. This plan for "school room libraries" was adopted in Buffalo and when it was put in force in New York City it was called "The Buffalo Plan." By right of priority, however, it was the Denver plan and a natural step in the developing program of its first librarian. A similar development arose out of the fact that the residents of Denver whom he employed had no previous training in library work. He adopted, therefore, the plan of taking in a class of apprentices in the fall who worked from six to nine months without compensation before they were put on the regular payroll. Carrying this program through two successive years, he had a staff of well-trained assistants, all thoroughly imbued with his own philosophy and methods.

He pushed his program of relating the library to definite

community needs in every direction. In the field of medicine he found a kindred soul in Dr. Henry Sewall. Together they worked out a plan by which the Colorado Medical Library Association and the Library co-operated in the purchase of medical journals and medical books. The consequent collection was much used. It marked the beginning of the Denver Medical Library.

In addition to its collection of books, the Library collected pictures from illustrated and art journals. This was a very early picture collection if not the first. More interesting than the gathering of pictures was his use of them. He worked with the director of the department of drawing in the schools in sending the illustrated magazines to the eighth grade teachers. With them he sent sheets of heavy paper. The teacher and pupils then selected the work of specified artists and mounted them. Arrangements of the pictures were then made either by artists or subjects. Biographical and critical notes were also preserved. In Dana's own words: "This opened the eyes of children and teachers to the artistic side of illustrative work. It brought home to them the fact that they have art at their very doors, if they will but enjoy it." As a further service to the community he kept the library open every day in the year from 9 A.M. to 9 P.M. for many years. Later it was closed on Christmas Day and July Fourth. By 1896 he could report that the number of volumes lent from the library averaged four per capita for the total population of the city. This compared with one in Providence, R. I., less than two in Newark, N. J., and three in Minneapolis, Minn.

In 1895, he was president-elect of the American Library Association and entertained its annual meeting in Denver. A visitor from Newark reported to a home-town paper: "All the meetings, except the first, were held at the Public Library, controlled by Mr. Dana, the next president of the association. This library is in the wing of one of Denver's High Schools. One feature particularly impressed me. In the reference department there was an herbarium filled with specimens of all the Colorado wild flowers, collected by the teachers and scholars of the city, and it was used just as one would use a book." In this same year, Dana wrote a pamphlet on Colorado in which he described its history, manufactures, agriculture and education. It is now chiefly remarkable as a reminder of the youth of this familiar state, for it was written while the early settlers were still alive enough to quicken a librarian's pen to such an opening paragraph as this:

The pioneer is the true prophet. He sees the farms, the villages, the cities that are yet to be. The new man, rejoicing in the new land, has a clear vision of the new world of prosperity and comfort his own energy is to create, and is thrilled thereby. He climbs every day his own delectable mountains and has every day a glimpse of the city of dreams which he will help to make real. Not all the men of push and energy, not all the men who wished to take part in the founding of new empires, have moved westward and still westward since Europeans first landed on this continent. But of those who have pushed westward by far the larger part have been touched at least with the colonizing zeal, have had in them the spirit of the pioneer, and have been possessed thereby with the vision of the seer.

Upon his election to the presidency of the American Library Association, Dana found himself dealing with wider issues than any he had heretofore confronted, and a note of regret at his being so far away from the main centers of population and activity began to creep into his letters. He wanted to be everywhere at once. In a single letter he says: "The library spirit is not yet born south of the Mason and Dixon line. How can the modern library idea be spread through the South?" and "I am giving so much advice, and doing so little comparatively myself that I begin to feel rather guilty." His work, however, was made easier by Mr. Elmendorf, Secretary of the A.L.A., of whom he writes: "Elmendorf is working day and night, as near as I can make out. He is firing letters at me by the score." Whatever Dana may have been prevented, by his isolation, from doing for the Annual Convention he made up by preparing a primer for librarians, designed to put into print his ideas of modern library practices. The annual meeting over which he was to preside was to be held in Cleveland. He was on pins and needles in anticipation of it. He wrote to his friend, Henry J. Carr of the Scranton, Pa., Library, telling of his fears that eastern people would think Cleveland too far west, and also of his perturbations over his own ability to preside—"my parliamentary law is rusty, my life so far from library centers has prevented my being familiar with the faces of A.L.A. members, and my Roman firmness is not apparent in my manner—I am a little afraid, especially if they have meetings of three or four hundred." Needless to say, his fears proved groundless and he carried off his duties as presiding officer with dignity and satisfaction.

His presidential address was aimed as a blow against all temptations to complacency. As he remarked: "I would wish to leave you, here at the very beginning of our discussions, not, indeed, in the Slough of Despond, but climbing sturdily, and well aware that you are climbing, the Hill Difficulty. Others, I can assure you, will, long before our conference ends, lead us again, and that joyfully, to our Delectable Mountains." He essayed to depict the social results of public library work as an accepted phase of political, that is, state activity. Calling attention to the fact that the organization of public schools had resulted in the almost complete transfer of responsibility for educating children from parents to the political unit with a conse-

quent decline of both parental direction and parental interest in what education was actually doing to the children,
he warned that the public library also might be merely
taken for granted and so become another agent of social
indifference, parents foregoing direct oversight over their
children's reading, and the loafers and the lazy passively
accepting the books presented to them. Against this poten-
tial tendency of the library to become merely another tax-
supported institution he warned his hearers vigorously. It
was not enough to run a place of apparent culture into
which the lazy and the bored come for refuge. "To produce
a maximum effect, even a desirable effect, the right books
must be put in the right hands at the right time." He drove
this home. "To the observant eye our libraries are not altogether halls of learning; they are also haunts of the lazy.
They do not interest parents in their children; perhaps
they lead parents to be indifferent to their children."

From this opening he pressed on to put the responsibility
for making the library a vital force squarely upon the
shoulders of the librarian. "A collection of books gathered
at public expense does not justify itself by the simple fact
that it is. If it be not a live educational institution it were
better never established. It is ours to justify to the world the
literary warehouse. A library is good only as the librarian
makes it so." He continued with a discussion of those attitudes that fit a librarian to make a library good. "Look first
to your own personal growth. . . . Broaden out." "Be social.
Impress yourself on your community, in a small way if not
in a large." "Speak out freely on matters of library management; and especially, in these days, on matters of library construction. . . . millions of dollars have been spent
on library buildings in this country, and we have not yet a
half dozen that do not disgrace us." "Advertise the A.L.A.
. . . Be ready to do the work to keep it properly alive and

well in the public eye." "Be not slow in giving hearty recognition to those who have taken the first place and borne the burdens and made an easy way for us who follow." "Interest in your work your local book-lovers and book-collectors and book-worms and private students and plodders and burners of the midnight oil."

He urged close co-operation with local book and news men, with teachers of literature, with women's clubs and art, historical and scientific societies, with clerygmen and institutions devoted to the service of youth. He laid great stress upon getting a knowledge of the library to business men and women: "Our work is but begun so long as we are not in close touch with the man of affairs." His final word was an exhortation to make the library a place sought out by men and women and children:

See that your library is interesting to the people of the community, the people who own it, the people who maintain it. Deny your people nothing which the book-shop grants them. Make your library at least as attractive as the most attractive retail store in the community. Open your eyes to the cheapness of books at the present day, and to the unimportance, even to the small library, of the loss of an occasional volume; and open them also to the necessity of getting your constituency in actual contact with the books themselves.

This was no address in the conventional pattern. It lifted above the threshold of discussion the differences that were dividing the traditional and the experimental librarians of the period. From the day of its deliverance its ideas have steadily gained dominance in the field of library administration. For this very reason, an address that was called radical then seems conventional enough now. It is the address itself which has helped the change.

His thinking about library buildings at this period was amplified in a paper which he read before the Colorado

Library Association on December 13, 1896. In it he made nine points clear. (1) The library is meant to serve not only as a place where books are kept, but also as a center of literary activity for the city, having rooms set aside for club meetings and lectures. (2) The library should be centrally located and the building planned for growth and economical administration. (3) There should be no unnecessary ornamentation for a library is neither an art gallery nor a museum. (4) Shelves should be open, with no shelf higher than a person of moderate height can reach. (5) Cases should be plain and should never cut off the light. (6) Natural light should be provided and artificial light reduced to a minimum. (7) There should be accommodations for readers near the books they want to use. (8) Separate rooms should be provided for newspapers, for magazines and periodicals, and for children's books. (9) The librarian should be accessible to the public and close to the delivery and catalogue rooms.

His ceaseless effort to take the library into the life of the community expressed itself in many exhibitions of the work done by the children and the schools, in an index of all the medical journals in the offices of Denver's physicians and a schedule of their availability for general use, and in his own active participation in communal societies and events. His love of print produced unusual catalogues and manuals of interpretation, and his love of debate made him a familiar figure wherever groups gathered to explore experience. He was an active member of the Artists' Club of Denver and chairman of its council for a time. He was still feeling his isolation from the chief library centers, however, so that when, in 1897, the Buffalo, N. Y., Library was looking for a "superintendent" he became an active candidate for the position. Frank P. Hill, then Librarian of the Newark Public Library, worked hard for his election, and

Frederick M. Crunden of the St. Louis Library gave him enthusiastic support. In the end, however, his A.L.A. colleague, H. L. Elmendorf, was elected to the position. Nathaniel W. Norton, president of the Buffalo Library Board, wrote Mr. Dana: "Your recommendations were all of the very best." Norton himself did not push Dana's candidacy because he was a classmate of Dana's at Dartmouth and as Frank P. Hill explained: "as he was the partial cause of Larned's resignation it might look like favoritism if he were to put in a Dartmouth man, and particularly a classmate, for Larned's successor."

This experience let the libraries of the East know that Dana was desirous of a change, and before the year was out he was invited to Springfield, Mass. and to Brooklyn, N. Y., in which latter city a new library was to be established. The Springfield election came first and though as he says he "flirted" with Brooklyn, he accepted the position of librarian of the City Library Association of Springfield. On November 20, 1897, he wrote to Samuel Bowles of the *Springfield Republican* a letter of acceptance in which he made a full confession of his "flirtation with the trustees of the Brooklyn Library . . . in order that you may understand it fully, and may have no reason from outside reports to think I have not been entirely straightforward with you and your people." When it was announced that he was leaving Denver there were expressions of high regard from many groups. His old friend, Frank E. Gove, called the Annual Meeting of the Dartmouth Alumni Association of the Great Divide at a special date to bid him, its president, farewell. Organizations that sent resolutions of regret to his board included the Woman's Club of Denver, Women's National Unitarian Alliance, City Improvement Society, Monday Literary Club, Denver Fortnightly Club, Artists Club, Colorado Library Association, and University of Denver. The Colorado Library Association included in its resolution the following tribute:

To him, as the moving spirit of the Colorado Library Association—its heart and soul—is due, more than to any other, the credit of its present standing, the good already accomplished, and its promising outlook for future usefulness in state library work.

Mr. Dana is a recognized authority in library matters, not only in Colorado, but in the East, and his withdrawal from the state would be seriously felt by the Public Library of Denver, by the Colorado Library Association, and by the entire library interest of this state. His personal and official influence is impressed upon them all.

Chancellor (later Bishop) William F. McDowell of the University of Denver added to the University's formal resolution his own personal appreciation:

I sent yesterday a properly signed request on behalf of the University of Denver for Mr. Dana's retention as Librarian, if it can be accomplished. I desire to add a personal word. I have not always agreed with Mr. Dana, but I cannot fail to see his efficiency as a librarian. He has made the library of the greatest possible use to our students, and I should count his removal as a great loss to the educational interests of the city.

On November 26, 1897 he submitted his formal resignation to take effect on December 31, and nominated Mr. John Parsons, his assistant, as his successor. In eight years and six months he had securely established both the Denver Public Library and his own reputation. He went to Springfield an acknowledged leader in his profession.

CHAPTER VI

SPRINGFIELD

WHEN Springfield looked at its new librarian it saw a man "tall and spare, with broad shoulders and a decided scholar's stoop. His face is strongly intellectual and earnest, but he has a winning smile and an attractive, pleasant manner."[1] His "scholar's stoop" was so characteristic of Mr. Dana that almost every description of him mentions it. His welcome to Massachusetts was assured by his name and origin. A Holyoke correspondent of the *Springfield Republican* wrote the editor in terms reserved by New England for its own sons. He assured his readers that Dana "comes of good Yankee stock, a descendant of the Cambridge Danas." The communication is worth quoting at more length as an illustration of Massachusetts as a state of mind:

The Danas married into the best families and have always been the leading family of Windsor County. The Dana store has been the leading, aristocratic, fashionable emporium for 95 years. . . . The whole Dana race have been scholars and lofty-minded people. They are, in Woodstock, the proper family, the finish of the upper round in the social scale of that aristocratic little burgh. . . .

His uncle Henry is the author of the history of Woodstock, a well-written book, which is in the Springfield city library. He is the finished scholar of Vermont and was chosen at an early age to select the Shakespearean quotations for Webster's Dictionary, as is mentioned in the preface of that work. The Danas have sent more of their members through the various colleges than any family in Vermont. Doctors, lawyers and reverends are indigenous to the blood.

Naturally, however, the advantage of his coming could not all be laid to one side. The *Boston Journal* tactfully sug-

[1] *Springfield Republican*, November 18, 1897.

gested that removal from Colorado to Massachusetts was bound to prove pleasing to Mr. Dana. In its issue of November 19, 1897 it declared: "Mr. John Cotton Dana . . . was one of the sound money advocates in Colorado who came very near to persecution because of his unwillingness to favor the free and unlimited coinage of silver at 16 to 1. A position in the Bay State must be acceptable after such an experience."

When Dana looked at Springfield he found himself confronted by a well established library, adequately equipped and operating in a secure tradition. Fresh from the adventure of founding an institution and setting its original patterns of work, he now had the more complex task of adjusting a going institution to his clear but not yet generally accepted convictions. The story of his Springfield work is largely one of transition. He made the library over into the image of his own thinking. It is a tribute both to himself and his Board of Trustees that he carried their approval as he made the changes. Dana began his duties at Springfield on January 1, 1898. He found the City Library Association maintaining an art museum and a museum of natural history as well as the library. A new art building had been built two years prior to his coming and a museum of natural history was in process of construction when he arrived. These extra activities were to his liking and he threw himself into them with enthusiasm.

He began immediately to fashion the library and its practices nearer to his heart's desire. Something there was in him that did not love a fence so he began to clear the library of all barriers. He removed the railings closing the alcoves in the main hall, thus making open shelves more easily accessible to the public. He took away the fence from the delivery desk to make the general appearance of the room more hospitable and to facilitate communication between the assistants and the public. He opened Sunday exhibits of illustrated books on certain given topics and so increased threefold the number of visitors on these days. Carrying into Springfield his passion for developing the love of books in children, he changed shelves to make it possible for children to have free access to books, and also for a children's corner to be arranged. He drove home to Springfield what he had stated again and again in Denver: "The early teens of boys and girls are the years in which they are most susceptible to influences of every kind, good or bad. . . . We have the strongest possible reasons for endeavoring to make the public library a co-worker with the public school; for endeavoring, through the public library, to acquaint children before they are 13 or 14 years old with the existence of the cheering and helpful things in good books, for endeavoring to encourage even the very young to form habits of good reading."

In addition to removing fences within the library, opening shelves to the public and giving the children a place of their own, he advocated making it easier for people to reach the library from the city. "The facts that the library is itself on a hill, and that its main reference room is reached from the street only by climbing three long flights of steps and stairs, probably seriously curtail its use and usefulness. An entrance from the level of the top of the first pair of outside steps into the basement, with an elevator to every floor, would add much to the convenience of the library for every one and for the older people particularly." He wanted a library of books for the people, with the latter finding it easy to get the reading they desired. Further to advance this aim he revised the shelving, classification and cataloguing of the books themselves. He also urged that the library become more closely affiliated with all the literary, scientific, historical and educational institutions of the community. "It must, as it grows, affiliate with itself more closely, and more diligently promote, all those movements which may in the broadest sense be called educational. The City Library is the people's college." In all he did he had the support of his Board. They saw that a librarian must be equipped not only with a knowledge of books but also with the art of making their use as free and far-reaching as possible. After four months of experience with the new librarian the Board expressed itself through the President at the Annual Meeting: "I need hardly tell you that the zeal with which Mr. Dana has entered upon the duties of the office and the masterful hand which he has already shown to us in grappling with the difficult problems of library work, are a significant augury for the growing influence and success of the institution."

From the multiplicity of duties in his new position, Dana took time out in the summer to visit Europe with his brother, Dr. Charles Dana. His letters indicate that while he was away Mrs. Dana began to suffer from "nerves" and took a violent dislike to Springfield. Troubled by her letters, Dana wrote to his brother, Joe, to provide for her, placing her in a suitable sanitarium for rest, if necessary. Meanwhile, he gave himself up to the joys of his first visit to the Old World. Edinburgh delighted him. He sat in the Princes Street Gardens, eating greengages and listening to the bewitching burr of the men of the North Country. He felt the keen air somewhat, but "between bagpipes and porridge" found the country had its joys. He visited North Berwick and played the links, but found the Bass Rock "one of the treats of the whole trip. I just don't know why."

On the links the two brothers met Sir Archibald Buchan Hepburn, a descendant of Bothwell. He invited them to spend a Sunday with him, and so they had the thrill of a day at a laird's house. John's enjoyment of the ample table they encountered leaves no doubt of the knight's hospitality. After another day spent on the St. Andrews links, the Danas were off to London and their journey was enlivened by the conversation of an ex-M.P. who did not quite approve of Gladstone because he was too socialistic. In London, John visited the Museum of the Geological Survey of Great Britain and secured the promise of material for an exhibit at Springfield. The travelers also had mutton at Simpson's.

Paris was taken in their stride and they visited the Casino at Aix-les-Bains. Dr. Charles had a patient of his convalescing at Annecy in Savoy. She had two relatives who were baronesses staying with her and John "rode between the two Baronesses!" on a drive through the mountains. He was all ears for their conversation about French life, and his eyes opened a bit wide apparently when they saw "fine ladies smoke cigarettes in the great court and corridors of the hotel."

Back at his work in Springfield, Dana plunged into a busy year of activities aimed at making his library a place inviting to people with all sorts of interests. The Museum of Natural History was opened on November 10, 1899, marking the climax of months of planning and effort. Meanwhile there were many exhibitions and lectures. The Art Museum showed a display of Photographs and Colored Prints of the Florentine, Umbrian and Lombard Schools, beginning with Cimabue and ending with Michelangelo. Mr. Henry W. Kent, "of the Slater Memorial Museum of Norwich, Connecticut," delivered a series of addresses on Greek and Renaissance Sculpture. There were three talks on Architecture, and an exhibition of Wood Engravings. Under the joint auspices of the Teachers Club and the City Library, Calvin Stebbins lectured on Oliver Cromwell and John Milton. Elbert Hubbard journeyed to Springfield to explain "The Work of the Roycrofters." The Free-hand Evening Drawing Classes had their own exhibition of drawings. And F. Schuyler Matthews lectured on "Wild Birds and Their Music." The program was active and varied, calculated to match the tastes of a cosmopolitan city.

The alumnae of the Catherine Howard School, as a memorial to Catherine L. Howard, raised several thousand dollars for the purchase of a science library and the establishment of a trust, the interest on which was to be used for additional purchases. Dana made their purchases the special library of the Museum of Natural History. He bought the books with the work of the schools especially in mind, carefully selecting them to meet the needs of both beginners and advanced students in the study of subjects covered by the collections in the museum: geology, physical geography, zoology, botany and astronomy. This type of work, matching institution specifically against institution for their mutual advantage, was the kind in which he was especially happy. He could already see teachers and students winding their way to the museum under this arrangement and it was good in his eyes.

Another instance of this linking of his institutions to already going organizations came when the library subscribed to, and made conveniently available for public use, the card-bibliography of zoology published by the "Concilium Bibliographicum" in Zurich, Switzerland. It covered Paleontology, Evolution, Microscopy, Preparation and Care of Zoological Specimens, Zoology and Physiology. This met a need felt by the Springfield Zoological Club, which expressed high appreciation for it in its report of October 1900. Here was another line from the library running to a specific group and its interests. As a matter of fact, this collection which totaled some 50,000 cards was the only complete one in New England, so that students from the colleges of the entire section found their way to the Springfield Library for this unique service. To get the library into the thinking of the whole community he sent circular letters to influential persons, either describing some activity or enlisting aid of some sort. The School principals were reminded of exhibitions of various kinds and asked to place prepared information about them in the hands of the appropriate teachers. Sunday School superintendents were informed of new books of value to their teachers, of collections of pictures illustrating the Old and New Testaments, and of special displays of pictures in the library itself illustrating chronologically such themes as the Life of Christ. Secretaries of organizations were asked to inform the librarian of their coming programs and to suggest books that would be of value, being assured that the library would prepare lists on special topics or would buy special books if desired. Clergymen were asked to assist in collecting data on the history of the city, and particularly to let the library have full information of their churches, including all publications. Such communications served a double purpose. They kept the library itself alive and they enlisted intelligent influence in important quarters.

He undertook to awaken the business men of Springfield to the value of their library in their work. His method was to speak personally with some three hundred men, not generally known to be either friendly or antagonistic to the library, and then to send them a communication asking for their replies to two questions, inferentially suggesting that these questions grew out of their conversations. The questions were: (1) What use do you make of the Public Library?, and (2) What changes in its management would make possible a larger use of the library by yourself or by others? These questions he also sent to thirty other librarians asking that they submit them in the same way to men in their communities, "to find out why the public library does not commonly interest the average business man."

Facing the same need for trained helpers that he had met in Denver, he inaugurated a library training class similar to the one he had conducted there. The course covered nine months during which the apprentices averaged 36 hours a week in the library without pay. Six young women were admitted to the first class. The professional interest behind this plan prompted him to call together the librarians of the neighboring parts of the State whom he organized into the Western Massachusetts Library Club. This group met regularly to discuss the problems and techniques of the library field, and provided an especially needed stimulus for the librarians of small libraries. It evidently aroused in Mr. Dana a curiosity about what librarians themselves were reading, for soon after its organization he sent a questionnaire to twelve librarians asking whether they were in the habit of reading Homer, Dante, Plato, Cervantes, Darwin, Goethe, Milton, Hugo, Bunyan, Bacon, Aristotle, Plutarch and Virgil. On the more practical side he devised a scheme for lessening the cost of printing catalogue cards and for simplifying the work of making a dictionary catalogue for a library.

One of Dana's kindling enthusiasms was for Japanese art. He could be persuaded to leave any beaten track if a Japanese print could be assured in a by-path. It is not surprising, therefore, to find him emphasizing an exhibition of Japanese art which he put into the library in 1898. The source of his joy in the work of the Japanese he expressed in the announcement of the display:

The first impression that many people, unused to Japanese art, gain from looking at it is that it is grotesque or "queer." After a very little study, however, anyone must begin to appreciate, and marvel at, the simple way that the Japanese artists take to say a great deal. A few well chosen oblique lines may give us the effect of a driving rain; or a light circle, surrounded by a delicate grey tone, may represent the feeling of evening.

On the other hand, in many drawings of birds and flowers, the exactness of detail would satisfy the scientist, while the result is highly artistic.

A little publication of another sort displayed a different side of Dana, his humor. It was called *The Complete Librarian* and was a playful attempt to stimulate his staff to do "the little more, and how much it is!" that would lift their work from mediocrity to distinction. The little pamphlet consisted of six pages with a woodcut on each and a legend using the picture as a text. For example, on one page was a picture of a cow and the legend read: "When the cow comes into the library, and seems to wish simply to browse, not to study, the librarian will put her out; the Complete Librarian will milk her first." He pointed similar parables with The Heron, Pocahontas, The Bull and The Light Fantastic.

Samuel Bowles, of the *Springfield Republican,* and a few kindred spirits had what Bowles described as "a talking club" which met once a month. They invited Dana to join them and so he shared in their conversational orgies while he lived in Springfield. The group included clergymen and doctors and editors, and among them was Mr. Gillette, then Congressman, later Speaker of the House of Representatives and United States Senator. Before this congenial company Dana read a paper on "Individualism" which showed him grappling with the recurrent question of the State and the individual. He used to call himself "a philosophical anarchist" and this paper was a comparatively mild declaration of his faith. Its thesis was summed up in these words: "An accompaniment of the progress of civilization has been the growth of individual liberty; perhaps that growth is civilization itself. We have no reason to suppose that more of liberty will not be a prerequisite to, or an essential part of, further progress."

An important possession, and one admirably suited to Dana's enthusiasm and purpose, came to the Springfield Library in 1899 when the David Ames Wells Economic Library and a bequest of $90,000 for the purchase of books in economics and the social sciences were given to it. After the necessary preliminaries of cataloguing and transferring the books were over, Dana completed the sets of journals and proceedings of societies already begun. Then he added all the books in Bowker and Iles' bibliography that were not present. He consulted Harvard College on the best books in economics published in the previous five years. He corresponded with the large libraries of the country on the scope and development of their economic departments. And then, as his own suggestion, he collected the best of the current novels dealing with economic questions and added these to the list. "It is hoped by this . . . to awaken an interest along these lines which will lead to a large and growing use of the collection." His administration of the Springfield Library producing a continually insistent change of the relation between the institution and the community attracted wide attention throughout the East. Librarians consulted him on matters of practice. Brooklyn again approached him to be its librarian. The New York Free Circulating Library invited him to take charge of its circulation department. Boston let it be known that it was considering him. To all suggestions of leaving Springfield he turned a deaf ear.

When the National Education Association, however, appointed a committee in 1899 to study the relation of public

libraries to public schools he was immediately interested
and accepted the chairmanship of the committee. The report which was produced reiterated the points of view
which Dana had expressed in Denver and in Springfield.
It emphasized that "the public library must, if it would
do good and not harm with its books, rely to a very great
extent upon the assistance of the schools." Of the librarian
it said: "She is always mindful that she is a public servant,
not a ruler; that she is a counselor, not a faultless guide;
that she is a student of books with the children as fellow-
students, not a teacher who has already learned all that
books can teach." Various practical suggestions were made
for completer service to the teachers by the library with
particular stress upon keeping teachers informed as to
special acquisitions by the library. Attached to the report
was a statement of working arrangements between libraries
and schools in certain typical communities. This report with
some supplementary material was published in pamphlet
form by the United States Bureau of Education in 1901.

In an article published over his own name in the *Journal
of Education*, Dana gave his own analysis of the basic reasons
for lack of co-operation between libraries and schools. He
stated them simply and somewhat severely: "The first is
the lack of the proper spirit in the librarian. . . . The other
is the small acquaintance the average teacher has with the
realm of printed things." He urged teaching directly aimed
at developing acquaintance with books as books. "High
schools, normal schools, colleges and universities do not as
yet pay much attention to the kind of book learning needed
if public libraries are to be effective helpers of the schools;
that kind which will be given when they have the long-
wished-for and long-hoped-for professorships of books." In
his annual report for 1899 he indicated that books need to
be supplemented by extra-literary objects: "The city li-

brary has added to Literature her proper companions, Art
and Science." He had gathered together a display of uten-
sils, "a collection of the products of the artist-artisan to bid
us all, as Morris would say, find pleasure in that which
we must perforce do and get pleasure from that which we
must perforce use." To these objects he had added a collection of reproductions of famous sculpture[1] and a collection of minerals and other natural products. He planned
for his books to lead to his objects and his objects back to
his books, and for the whole library to become "each
year more and more the central point of the scientific,
literary and artistic life of the city."

While in Denver Mr. Dana had written *A Library Primer*.
It was published serially as six articles in *Public Libraries* in
1896. In 1899 he revised, rewrote and extended these articles and they were published in book form by the Library
Bureau. It was what its name implied, and was definitely
aimed at correlating library knowledge for the use of librarians of small libraries. A second edition was published
in 1909 and a complete revision in 1920. It has taken its
place as the classic description of library procedures, basic
to the whole work of the profession of the librarian. There
were two convictions that balanced each other in his thinking, one that the library had an educational and moral
service to perform, and the other that it must be a center
of public happiness catering to the demands and even to
the whims of the public. It was not always easy to yoke
these two theories so as to make them pull together. He
emphasized both in the *Primer*, and came back to a discussion of them in a letter to *The Springfield Republican* on
November 13, 1899. Speaking of the books "everyone is
reading" he wrote: "The librarian sees them come . . .
and, alas, he sees them go. . . . They line his shelves; they

---

[1] Provided by funds derived from the estate of Horace Smith.

gather dust; their titles fill his catalogs; . . . what, then, should the librarian do? . . . he says to himself 'I will be stern and will buy for this library only the best novels and few of them.' . . . Then he considers further and finds that the library is the public's and who, then, is the librarian that he should do other than the things the constant reader may approve?" He solved the riddle by insisting that even the argument for entertainment leads back to the best books and that mere uninformed demand is no justification for pulling the library down to a second- or third-rate level. He summed up his conclusion: "[The librarian] considers the many libraries of moderate size which offer a selection of 5,000, 6,000, or even 9,000 titles in novels and remains firm in his conviction that . . . two thirds or more must be weak, silly and third-rate, for there are not 2,000 good novels yet put into print. He believes that the claims of literature, of education and of sound economy are all on the side of the conservative course in novel buying."

In the closing days of 1899 Mr. Dana presented in the Art Building an exhibition of 150 pictures of Oliver Cromwell and his noted contemporaries and of scenes and incidents of his time. This was in celebration of the tercentenary of the Lord Protector's birth. It drew an unusually large attendance. To supplement the display the City Library issued a handsome pamphlet *The Cromwell List*, containing a bibliography on Cromwell, an original estimate of him by Arthur Paterson, author of *Cromwell's Own*, tributes to him from English writers and 20 illustrations especially made for this publication. This enterprise illustrated one method Dana followed to win people to the reading of the more substantial books. In his preface to *The Cromwell List* he wrote: "This little book is the outcome of an effort to limit the library's purchases to fiction of the first class; and of an effort at the same time to in-

crease the interests in books other than fiction among habitual readers old and young." In the words of *The Springfield Republican* (March 8, 1900): "Under the vital and
constant activity of Mr. Dana, the university of the people,
. . . is rapidly increasing its activity;" the city was discovering "in what multitudinous ways the City Library is
capable of contributing to, strengthening and broadening
the community's life." In an article of about the same date
Dana picturesquely expressed the point of view that lay
back of the effects the *Republican* described: "The library
of the future will not only have a corner for the grocers. It
will have corners also for the plumbers, the sanitary engineers, the carpenters and the builders, and for all the trades
and callings prominent in the community." This kind of
concrete thinking was the stuff out of which roads were
built from workshops and offices to the library.

During this same period Dana wrote a long article on
Woman's Suffrage in Colorado which was published by
the *New York Times* and the *Boston Transcript*. He pointed
out that the right to vote had transformed neither the
women nor the politics of Colorado. His views aroused a
wide discussion, but perhaps the most diverting comment
was made by Mrs. L. M. Stansbury of Colorado Springs
who took the opportunity to describe Dana himself as she
knew him: "Fascinating, entertaining, delightful,—Mr.
Dana is all of this, but no one, in their wildest moments,
ever accused him of being enthusiastic. It is doubtful if
there are a dozen persons in the United States who believe
in fewer things than John Cotton Dana. It was whispered
during his residence in Denver that he never voted at all,
and, so far as political affiliations were concerned, that he
had none whatever, being what is known as a 'philosophical anarchist.' Just what that may be is uncertain, but it
seems to mean a person who does not believe in govern-

ment." Alice Stone Blackwell seized upon this to remark "that Mr. John Cotton Dana, though a very amiable gentleman, is understood to be a philosophical anarchist, not believing in suffrage for either man or woman; his views of what women can accomplish with the ballot are naturally influenced by his general opinions." Whatever his doubt of the efficacy of political methods in general Dana spoke strongly on public questions. He wrote a vigorous letter condemning what he called "McKinley and his empire": "It should be gall and wormwood to those who have fallen into this hysteria of empire, conquest and christianizing that the fit was induced largely by the sentimental and maudlin and insensate ravings of a few of the least respected and least responsible of our newspapers. . . . We have at Washington a strictly 'money' government, established by money, sustained by money, to be perpetuated by money, and always and forever for money at every turn. And consider the carnival of joy among those who are profiting by the $250,000,000 of taxes taken for war from a prosperous and hypnotized people almost within a twelvemonth."

While these affairs of the great world commanded his pen he could still turn his hand to humbler tasks. On one occasion some ladies had decorated the Museum of Natural History with flowers and ferns. When they had finished there was the natural debris of stems and leaves upon the floor. They approached an assistant to have the floor swept. The cleaning women were busy so the assistant asked Mr. Dana to direct them to leave what they were doing and to sweep the floor. As Dana described it: "She said the ladies wished the floor swept up at once. I asked her if she could not do it herself and she flatly refused. I went over there with a broom and with the help of the ladies swept up the floor."

An article in *Art Education* for May 1900 gave him a

chance to expound again his love of good printing: "All of the library's printing, if means and opportunity permit (and the cheapest of printing can show good taste to some extent) should be done with a view to its possible influence on design in general and on good printing in particular. Not many people as yet appreciate the fact that the simplest piece of printing is, or may be, either good or bad in design. Few printers consider this at all. The library can do much to attract attention to this subject by giving attention to its printing."

In his annual report he posed the main question before the public library as it developed: "The question once was, 'What can the library be?' Today it is, 'What can the library do?' Formerly it was a question of resources, of number of books, of wealth of material. Now it is rather a question of effectiveness, of vitality, of influence on community." This brought him back to his perpetual problem of how to govern his purchases. He was faced by demands created by "the passing craze, the notorious individual, the episodes of the times . . . politics, money questions, socialism, faith cure, higher criticism, Mansfield, Dreyfus, Zola, Ibsen, the Philippines, Boers, child-study, Tissot, automobiles, Paris, China, and the Nicaraguan canal." Yet he felt the library must "stand a little on its dignity" and not load itself down with books soon outdated. He resolved his dilemma in part by charging at the rate of two cents a day for books in large demand that otherwise appeared to have too transitory an interest to warrant their purchase in any quantities. Discussing why children should read the good old books he gave it as his opinion that they "should know of them as they hear of streams, and the woods, and the streets, and the playgrounds, and the kind men and women about their homes. In due course the children should meet them, and find them pleasant, and learn to know them,

and to love them. This is the beginning of 'literature.' "
As an example he told of "a half-dozen inquisitive little
Poles for three successive Sundays turned away from the
library because their faces and hands did not seem worthy
to meet with Mother Goose; the fourth Sunday they came
clean and humble, but still eager."

During the summer he took a trip to Canada and wrote
the *Springfield Republican* a letter describing "Two of Canada's Oldest Cities, Montreal and Quebec." Montreal, he
described, as a city without unity, divided between two
discordant peoples, the French and the English; Quebec,
however, was a city with a heart and soul, having a personality as distinct as any city in this western continent can
hope to attain for many years to come. "What a pity that
Canada and the Canadians are not of us. . . . If we wish
something to conquer here is a conquest worth making.
A half-score years of unhindered communion with our Ca-
nadian fellow-continentals would make them ours in heart
if not in name—and of what value then would be the
name?"

On his return he checked on the books that people read.
His conclusion, after compiling the list of those most frequently borrowed, was: "From lists like this no definite
conclusions can be drawn . . . unless the following—that
people are inclined to read, outside of fiction, a fairly
wholesome class of literature; that they like to be entertained and informed; but that they evade with considerable care anything that would tend to lead them to think."

Part of his own reading, necessarily, consisted of book
reviews. One day he decided to become a critic of the
critics and wrote a letter to the *Republican* on the failure of
book reviewing. He declared that a librarian could get little helpful information from most reviews. They contained
almost no information about the paper used, the binding,

the index, the margins or the full-page illustrations. More seriously, they could not be relied upon for genuine evaluation of the books' contents. "Every new book they mention is excellent . . . an Augustan Age comes round again with every rising sun." To support his statements he analyzed reviews from *The Critic, The Bookman, The Bookbuyer* and *The Nation*. Of 75 reviews in *The Critic*, 40 gave high praise and 15 some praise. In *The Bookman* the figures ran 54, 39 and 9; in *The Bookbuyer*, 60, 31 and 20; in *The Nation*, 54, 31 and 8. He added a little acid to his general comment by pointing out that *The Bookman* and *The Bookbuyer* were publishers' organs so that they could hardly be expected to do anything "but praise their own books and for the sake of peace refrain from condemnation of those of other publishers." The gauntlet thus thrown down was quickly seized upon. The letter itself was widely quoted and the inky hosts were arrayed in two opposing armies. One critic frankly took the position that "a sympathetic attitude toward life and literature is the best attitude for all critics to cultivate." Another pointed out that few books are wholly good or wholly bad, and that if a book has strong points the critic must notice and praise them. The editors of *The Critic* wrote an open letter to Mr. Dana. They seized on one sentence in his original letter which read, "Of the purely literary journals like *The Critic* which must support itself largely by advertising in one column the books which it professes to criticize with unbiased mind in the next, it is perhaps seeking grapes of thorns to demand unterrified censure." This sounded to the editors like an accusation of blackmail. They particularly disliked his suggestion that *The Nation* was doing a fairer job of adequate reviewing. Mr. Dana made the neat reply: "My article is one of the few things of which in recent years *The Critic* has thoroughly disapproved and which has been admitted to the distinction of a notice in its columns." The *Evening Telegram* of New York reviewed the whole battle and summed up its conclusion: "On the whole it's a very pretty row, and Mr. Dana seems to have rather the better of it." One amusing postscript to this experience was a complaint from *The Dial* that it had been omitted from the reviews analyzed.

A few weeks later Hamilton Wright Mabie had an editorial in *The Outlook* on "Modern Pagans." It was a plea that modern men should not neglect "the spiritual life" in their absorption in physical well-being; and it attributed spiritual idealism largely to the influence of Christianity. Dana thought he detected a note of complacency in it, and sent Mabie a frank letter: "Your article is aimed, with evident design, rather to give comfort and a feeling of self-gratulation to professing Christians than to arouse contrition in the minds of those who are 'not as they are, thank God.' Your editorial is designed to promote professional smugness." In a private paper Dana wrote: "The broad world holds no pagans for me. . . . To each man is one pagan only, to be found in his own secret heart. . . . Do I wish to become a missionary to the heathen? Let me visit the by-ways of my own conscience."

As 1900 turned into 1901 Dana was visited by a call to leave Springfield. The New York City Library invited him to become superintendent of circulation and organizer of branch libraries. Samuel Bowles put pressure on him to stay where he was: "If there is anything I can do or say to keep you from going, I want to do and say it. We cannot spare you." On January 1, 1901, Dana wrote to Dr. John S. Billings: "After much careful consideration I have decided to say that I cannot consider the suggestion you make in regard to the position in New York."

A year later Vice Chancellor James E. Howell and Mr.

Richard C. Jenkinson of the Library Board of the Newark
Public Library visited Dana and persuaded him to accept
the position of Librarian in Newark, N. J. When he announced his resignation from the Springfield position there
was wide criticism of its Board for allowing him to leave.
Even the *Boston Herald* joined the chorus. The decision,
however, was his own. Many letters came to him from his
associates praising his work. More highly prized, however,
were those in which his personal friends of Springfield days
spoke touchingly of their affection for him. Charles D.
Reid wrote: "We love you and need you, and I feel that
some way must open to keep you." Even more eloquent of
the sincerity of this general feeling of personal loss at Dana's
going was a letter written by Bowles to another friend, and
never intended for Dana's eyes: "I do not cease to mourn
the departure of our friend Dana. It really seems as if a
light had gone out in my own daily life." The *Springfield
Republican* concluded its comment upon him with the words:
"Mr. Dana has done his work well and it will stand."

The four years Dana spent in Springfield reintroduced
him to the East and particularly to the ways of New England. Apparently the environment awakened echoes of his
early training and renewed inner conflicts that he had
thought resolved forever. The West had emancipated him
from some of the old controls, but it had not entirely de-
stroyed them, for when he returned to New England they
began to stir again. He had to fight once more his own
inner battle for the freedom of his thought from the insist-
ent conventions of this more crystallized community. He
won the struggle but the conflict, while it was raging, made
him almost pugnacious in his resistance to opposition of
any kind from others. This was aggravated by the fact
that Mrs. Dana did not take the change of residence pleasantly. She developed a hypochondriac tendency as an ex-

cuse for herself and as a demand for attention. In addition,
certain older officers of the Library and Museum, in whom
years of incumbency created an illusion of infallibility, resisted his experimentation and sometimes thwarted his
plans.

Privately, therefore, the Springfield years were not his
most pleasant ones, and it was natural that he should seek
respite from private cares in public controversy. He pursued these disputes to the bitter end, in some cases until
editors, including his friend Bowles, had to refuse him
further space. Hamilton Mabie's article acted as a precip-
itant for this whole period. It spoke the familiar language
of his childhood. It awakened echoes of the old imperatives and made him furious. When he had thought and
lived through it, however, he had grown into a new stage of
conscious self-mastery. It was a relief to go to Newark, but
it was more. It was a chance to test his new sense of power.
A new chapter in his own growth was beginning and a new
field was its symbol. When Dana turned his face toward
Newark in January 1902 he had within him experiences
gained in two differing library fields. To the pioneer experiences of Denver he had added those of reorganizing a
well established library and at the same time of having
under his authority museums of art and natural history.
He was fully equipped to meet the city into which his re-
maining years were to be poured and with which his name
will always be most closely associated.

CHAPTER VII

THE LIBRARIAN AND HIS LIBRARY

JUST before Mr. Dana's arrival the City of Newark had built its present Public Library facing Washington Park. Frank P. Hill was the librarian and he had made the city sufficiently conscious of the importance of its library to spend $425,000 on this beautiful and commodious building. With Beatrice Winser, his assistant librarian, he had transferred the collections of books to their new home. So Mr. Dana moved at once into the building and the office where he was to spend his remaining and most productive years.

The trustees had made a courageous selection. Newark is not a city hospitable to experimentation. The solid conservatism of its Puritan founders has never been dissipated. At the turn of the century, religious orthodoxy and social acceptance were strongly fortified in the two powerful establishments of Old First Church and Trinity Church. These were rich and powerful centers of influence, sufficiently strong to check any untoward impulses to change. The men who invited Dana, acquainted as they must have been with his restless opinions, gave evidence of unusual independence. Within the library, where his work was more thoroughly known, his coming was anticipated with no little apprehension. Mr. Hill wrote to him asking him to leave at least the foundations of the library intact. The members of the staff openly wondered what "this radical" would do to their beloved institution. Behind the dignified welcome extended editorially by *The Newark Evening News*, the people in the know awaited the newcomer with some trepidation.

All that most people knew was that a new librarian had come to town. Their first approach to any knowledge of him was in his professional activity; and his first task was to learn and to lead the work of the library. He made no changes in the staff. Beatrice Winser continued to be assistant librarian throughout his administration. He took the experts whom he found, acknowledged their gifts and won them to full co-operation in his aims and methods. He early defined what he set out to do. Speaking at Indianapolis in the year following his arrival in Newark he expressed it thus:

Newark is a manufacturing city . . . thirty minutes and ten cents from New York; consequently most of its artistic, literary, scientific and musical, and much of its financial and social interest, centres there. . . . The city has no art gallery, no museum of natural history, no music hall worthy of itself, no adequate art school, no sufficient technical school and joins with the State in permitting the historical library to languish for lack of funds.

Now, in any community which has not the institutions and interests which I have mentioned, what should be the attitude of the free public library:

1. We should make ourselves in effect a part of all the school work of the city, public and private.
2. We should aid in such work as schoolroom decoration.
3. We should help to establish a museum of science.
4. We should help the local musical interests.
5. Study clubs, literary, artistic or musical, it is, of course, our function to aid by all means at hand.
6. We should help charitable organizations of all kinds like those working for vacation schools, which originated in Newark many years ago, for summer playgrounds and kindred organizations.
7. We should develop an interest in art, both fine and applied.
8. Every city is capable of betterment in streets, parks, schools, public buildings, monuments, drives, cleanliness and sanitation, and we should play our part.

Such a program, widely conceived as it was, had to be worked out within the technical framework of his institution. So it was quite natural that his mind should be occupied with the definition of his professional responsibilities and of his relationships with those who, with him, were responsible for the conduct of the library. On this latter point he set forth clearly the division of labor between the librarian and his trustees:

(The) librarian should have control of building and employees. Employees, of course, have the right of appeal to the trustees and other high authorities. . . .The general outline of the management of the library, its books and the building itself, have been determined by the trustees, the whole matter should be carried out by the librarian. The librarian, of course, will find it wise to interpose the trustees and the general rules they establish between himself and the public in the case of a public library, and between himself and the students in the case of a college library, but the librarian's position should be akin to that of the manager of a manufacturing establishment or of a railway. Individual trustees should never interfere. Trustees as a body . . . outline policy.

Turning to his immediate responsibility for the purchase and distribution of books he wrote down seven rules for his own guidance. It is an interesting comment on his meticulous self-discipline that these statements are specific, categorical and brief. He may have come a long way from the theology of his forbears, but their habits of control were ingrained in him. The standards he set himself were:

1. Buy of recent novels only a few.
2. Buy of no novel until it has been out a year or more.
3. Put all recent novels on the list tentatively only, and drop them if time does not prove them good.
4. Spend less money on fiction.
5. Spend the money thus saved on duplicates of other good books.
6. If a reduction in the list of novels reduces the cost of maintenance, spend the money thus saved in attracting readers to other books.
7. Reduce the formality of book-borrowing still further, following recent commercial methods, and secure a larger number of borrowers.

We cannot doubt that these rules had to be modified in practice, for he had a profound conviction that the library existed to serve the people and not as a proving ground for the librarian's predilections, but they set his main course.

When he interpreted his work in his annual report of 1903 he began by emphasizing the possibilities of the public library for civic usefulness as his main point of reference. Around it he organized his suggestions that the information desk should become a familiar and competent source of facts for all enterprises and individuals; that special cases of books should be displayed plainly marked in such ways as "Interesting Books," "One Hundred of The Best Novels," "One Hundred Biographies," "Books On Business"; that more liberal provisions for borrowing books be adopted; that a more active co-operation between library and public schools be established; and that the library lead in demonstrating the value of pictures in education. *The School Review* commented editorially on this discussion: "One lays down this report with a sense of gratification that there are men who realize the possibilities of their professions, and who point out the way to the many thousands to whom the work is only a trade involving mastery of details."

One kind of situation with which a librarian is often confronted is that in which groups of people, often for reasons undoubtedly moral in their eyes, object to certain books appearing on the shelves or being circulated. Dana was no censor, and never allowed himself to seem such for a moment. In 1905 the New York Public Library placed certain of Shaw's books on the restricted list. The inevitable reporter asked Shaw for his opinion of this action. He, nothing loathe, swung into verbal combat, storming thus:

Before you undertake to choose between evil and good in a public library or anywhere else, it is desirable that you should first learn to distinguish one from the other. The moment you do that, say, after forty years' study of social problems, you realize that you cannot make omelettes without breaking eggs; that is, you cannot have an advance in morality until you shake the prevailing sense of right and wrong sufficiently to compel a readjustment. . . . I do not say that my books and plays cannot do harm to weak or dishonest people. They can and probably do. But if the American character cannot stand that fire even at the earliest age at which it is readable or intelligible, there is no future for America.

This was a trumpet in Dana's ears and he joined the charge: "I commend to my fellows Bernard Shaw's letter. Far be it from me to find fiendish pleasure in his burning words! They apply to no particular librarian but to the whole Sweet Branch of Very Pure Librarians." He simply could not stand the kind of professional pose that was no more than a cloak for complacency and, even worse, timidity. The supercilious smile of condescension, that curves the lips of some who find their only satisfaction in patronizing those whom they are set to serve, was not only not for him, its mere presence in the neighborhood made his blood run hot. He pleaded for "bibliothecal skepticism." "After an institution is well on its way its greatest peril lies in self-content. . . . In the day of its youth it suddenly takes on the repose of old age. . . . It needs to search tirelessly for the new, to question at every point, to try all things, to doubt; to cultivate, in a word, bibliothecal skepticism."

In the address which he delivered at the A.L.A. meeting in Portland, Ore. in 1905 he went still further into the place of the library in the social structure, discussing its organization and its professional associations in their relations to the whole democratic idea:

To work with your fellows to a common end—this is to be civilized, to be moral, to be efficient. This makes nations possible and promises the parliament of the world.

And so, in speaking of associations of librarians, the first thing to be said is that they effect so much by the mere fact that they are. . . . One may well say, then, that the best work of an association is the association itself.

Remember that, after all, if you wish a certain thing done you must do it yourself. The crowd has the passing emotion, the one man has the tireless zeal. Don't think an organization is an end. . . . We can't conquer the public with our clubs. Moreover, never let your association hamper its strongest members. Democracy is the apotheosis of mediocrity. If the many would advance they must look to the leader to guide them. In union is strength; but the worth of strength is in its use. An association must guard against a tendency to the academic, and to holding its members to a standard, often a narrow one.

This protest against narrow professional standards rigidly enforced was no sign of lack of pride in his profession itself. Because he honored it he tried to make it more aware of its backgrounds and possibilities. He sought to lift its horizons on all sides. Accordingly, in 1906 he collaborated with Mr. Henry W. Kent, then librarian of The Grolier Club, in the preparation for publication of a series of six reprints of rare and out-of-print 17th and 18th century works on libraries and their management. All of them were printed in English, some of them being now translated for the first time. A. C. McClurg published and The Merrymount Press printed them. They included:

i. Cotton Des Houssayes, Jean Baptiste (1727–1783)
   Concerning The Duties And Qualifications of A Librarian.
ii. Drury, John (1596–1680)
   The Reformed Librarie-Keeper. (London, 1650)
iii. Kirkwood, Reverend James (1650–1708)
   An Overture for founding and maintaining of Bibliothecks in every Paroch throughout this Kingdom. (Edinburgh, 1699)
iv. Lipsius, Justus (1547–1606)
   De Bibliothecis Syntagma. (Antwerp, 1602)

v. Bodley, Sir Thomas (1545–1613)
> *Life, written by himself,* 1609; with his *First Draught of the Statutes of the Public Library at Oxford.*

vi. Naudé, Gabriel (1600–1653)
> *News from France, or, Description of the Library of Cardinal Mazarin.* (London, 1652)

The numbers sold were few although the *New York Times* reviewed these volumes enthusiastically, ascribing their origin to "that enthusiastic and militant librarian, John Cotton Dana."

Turning to another side of his profession, he urged his colleagues to know the technical manufacturing of books. "Those who work among books find it worth while to become familiar with their physical features. . . . For this paper I select 40 things as especially worthy of study. . . . My suggestion is that library assistants select one of these topics for study, and, in the course of the study, rather as a basis of it, make a collection of specimens; and that they carefully mount and arrange these specimens." His list includes book papers, water-marks, printing inks, lining papers, book covers, type faces, title-pages, and similar features.

Meanwhile, within his own library, he was continually trying experiments, stimulating his assistants, and devising plans to bring more and more kinds of people within the library's circle of service. After five years there was much to report. Newark has a substantial jewelry industry, so Dana gathered an exhibit of books relating to jewelry trade and manufacture, with illustrations of the work of some of the most famous artisans; and he told the jewellers he had it. He followed it up with collections of a similar sort for builders, leather manufacturers, architects, and other groups. When Mme. Sarah Bernhardt visited the city, he displayed books, pamphlets and pictures of French drama.

In response to many questions brought to the Library from the schools and others interested he actively inaugurated a formal study of the history of Newark, in which little, prior to his time, had been done. The halls of the library were thrown open to clubs so that their members might learn the way there. One highly successful venture was a collection of art from the homes of residents of the city; it made the city aware for the first time of its own possessions. Within Newark are large numbers of Germans, Russians, Poles, Italians and Hungarians; Dana accordingly brought together the best books he could find in these languages. He was continually giving his staff informal instruction, and they caught his spirit so that as many as fifty organizations at once were pursuing studies aided by staff-members. The reference desk was also emphasized, so that its telephone was continually in use to answer the varied questions coming from people in all walks of life who had learned how to use their library. So highly individualized a person as Dana naturally resisted any move which might seem to restrict his unhampered administration of his institution. It is not strange, therefore, to find him opposing the subjection of libraries to the civil service law. He had no love for boards sitting in another city laying down rules for his work, and the idea that promotion in rank or pay should be "automatic" violated every principle of spontaneity and experimentation by which he worked. He was vigorous in opposition, but ultimately the libraries came under the law.

More to his liking was the organization of the Special Libraries Association. At Bretton Woods on July 2, 1910 he proposed and outlined its organization, and was elected its first President. The "special libraries" for which it was designed were municipal, technical, legislative, reference, commercial, and public welfare libraries. Thirty years of active experience have proved the validity of his proposal. His interest in special libraries was more than academic, for, as the pioneer, he had established a business branch of the Newark Library in a room on the ground floor of a building at the center of the business section of the city. Here he gathered directories, selected government publications, manufacturers' catalogs, railway folders, local city and state pamphlets, and books on accounting, advertising, business management, and the like. He was particularly interested in the maps which formed part of the collection and its service.

When the tenth anniversary of his appointment came around he could point to the fact that he had transferred to the Newark Library all of the innovations that had approved themselves in his previous work. He could also justly claim that the Library itself had attained a new magnitude in the life of the city. Within the institution he had the devoted support of his staff who, to the last individual, had been completely won over by his disarming attitude and his obvious power.

As his work progressed, he found an excellent division of responsibility established between himself and his assistant librarian, Beatrice Winser. Mistress of detail, inexhaustible in energy, forthright in expression, yet fully conscious of his superior gifts and his prerogatives, she took from his shoulders much of the routine organizational work; thus leaving him free to write, to plan policies and to devise new plans. He taught her much but he leaned upon her heavily. Together, they formed a team in which the gifts of each supplemented those of the other most admirably. In ten years they had raised the number of books lent by the Library from 323,000 a year to over a million.

One effective method followed by Dana for stirring the interest of his fellow-citizens was the monthly publication which he called *The Newarker*, and which, in addition to news of the Library, carried special articles on Newark life. It demonstrated his theory: "I believe there is more inspiration to civic decency for a child in the story of how his community gets a supply of pure water than there is in the best fairy tale ever devised or the noblest Teutonic myth ever born." In 1914 he edited a series of pamphlets on "Modern American Library Economy, as illustrated by the Free Public Library of Newark." These were published by The Elm Tree Press in his native town of Wood-stock, Vermont. This press had been established by his brothers and was run by them; it was the projection in his father's store of the little printing machine on which as a boy he had run off *The Acorn*.

An old question came to him from E. R. Perry, Los Angeles Librarian, who asked his opinion of setting up turnstiles to keep people from stealing books. He still did not like fences: "Tell the people it is theirs to pay the quite minor cost of theft of books, this being the price they pay for a certain hospitable air which the library possesses." In April 1915 he returned to the charge on another of his old battlefronts with an address on "Paid Advertising For Libraries." He had lost none of his enthusiasm for it. He suggested that the libraries of America form a "Library Advertising Association," and put on a big national advertising campaign, using page space in a few big weeklies and monthlies.

His increasing reputation brought him many invitations to speak at dedications of new libraries and at many civic gatherings. Among other groups, the International Meeting of Librarians asked him for a paper at their meeting in Oxford in November 1914. In 1916 The H. W. Wilson Company published some of these productions of his in the book: *Libraries: Addresses and Essays by John Cotton Dana, a book of addresses delivered by Mr. Dana, the first in 1896 and the last in 1915.* It was about this time, also, that he composed the legend now carved in oak and hung over the vestibule entrance of the Rochester Public Library:

THE LIBRARY GATHERS LEARNING FOR LEARNING'S INCREASE;
SETS OPINION FREE THAT TRUTH MAY PREVAIL;
AND ASKS ALL MEN TO SEEK FOR WISDOM.

The coming of the war plunged him into discouragement. He felt that the war mania was a comment on the futility of his work. "The war has shown us that we are quite uncivilized. . . . When Mars is talking, books have to sit still. Librarians cannot prevent the breakdown of civilization! . . . The library, like the school, is merely an unimportant by-product of a certain stage of invention, discovery and social arrangement. . . . The site for the useful library edifice we hope to build is right in the center of poor human nature, and this center is now a morass of greed, servility, prejudice, national hatred, and general beastliness." He kept himself free, however, from war hysteria and never yielded to the demand that German books be taken from the library shelves. One metropolitan paper attacked him by name for it. Another sent a reporter to get a statement, implying that it would call him to account for his stand. Their young man was shown the door by one of the trustees of the Library, Mr. J. Henry Bacheller, who sent him off with the warning: "Don't attempt to threaten us!" Nevertheless, these were years that bore heavily on Dana's heart as he saw all he had anticipated falling away before him. He also faced the immediate problem of the closing of six branches, compelling the main Library to house 40,000 more books.

When the war was over, he recovered his spirits and was soon back planning new lines of work. He put out 44 leaflets treating of Newark's varied aspects, such as the County

Park System, Police Department, City Noises, Juvenile Delinquency, Care of the Insane, and similar topics. He also announced a scheme for indexing and cross-indexing the whole field of fiction. Under "Country Rustic," for example, would be found Ichabod Crane, Sam Slick, Squire Western, and Horseshoe Robinson. "The Saintly Child" would introduce Little Eva and Little Nell, as well as Little Lord Fauntleroy, who might also be found under "Juvenile Prig." At the request of the United States Shipping Board, he also compiled lists of books on world trade, foreign countries, foreign languages, and the merchant marine. In an entirely different field, he prepared an exhibit on the value of studying Latin, based upon Professor Frances E. Sabin's book *The Relation of Latin to Practical Life,* and this travelled to many schools and colleges, including Dartmouth and Princeton.

One innovation that he developed in 1918 is worthy of more than passing notice. It was the filing of pamphlets by the color band method. The printing presses were pouring out so many pamphlets that it was next to impossible to file them advantageously. Dana wrestled with this difficulty and devised a method which, with subsequent modifications, has established itself as the most convenient one proposed. "The gist of my answer lies in two things: Use the ordinary vertical file for current swiftly changing things; and use colored paper bands pasted on their backs to distinguish one from the other the pamphlets which stand closely ranked on ordinary shelves. This latter suggestion I believe to be quite revolutionary. . . . The bands can be not only of several colors, but also in several positions, each position being as distinguishing a mark as is the color itself; the bands can be changed in meaning by giving them differences in width; and by giving to ten different colors the values of the nine digits and zero."

When the moving pictures began to demand the time of people, Dana arose as a champion of the book against its new competitor. "The movie," he wrote, "was born almost in the mud of the world's first seas. . . . To attend a movie is to be primitive; to attend a lecture is to be a cave man; to read is civil." This started a merry row. Himebaugh and Browne, booksellers and publishers, sent out the inevitable questionnaire to educators and psychologists. Dana did not bow to the storm. In his annual report he said: "The growth of the habit of reading has been checked by the movies; but it has nevertheless continued, and at a very rapid rate." He kept hammering away at the necessity for the library's accelerating this growth of the reading habit. "It is the library's purpose to try to see itself as it really is; to note where it stands in relation to all the activities of the typical city that supports it, and to make itself of use to that city, freely modifying its work, and changing and extending its field as frank inquiry suggests."

As he saw science advancing in its control and modification of man's environment, he asked himself the question: What does this mean for the library? His answer was clear:

Science and technology have revolutionized the externals of life in the last 50 years. The inner life of man has, however, remained much the same. . . . Now, granted that the nature of man, his tendency to prejudice and his easy surrender to the baser passions, can be changed but slowly—very, very slowly; still we may venture to be a little hopeful, and may permit ourselves to believe that were knowledge of what scientific studies have disclosed to us more widely spread, more fully accepted, and more sharply felt, we should have thereby a cheering assurance of more of peace and less of war in this sad world. The suggestion which thereupon follows is this: that libraries exercise more freely the right which their very existence gives them of being tactful distributors of all that scientific study has discovered, and thereby induce more citizens to become acquainted with, and ultimately friendly to, first, the method of science, and next, those facts about human origins and the development of society which study has brought forth in the last few decades.

We can do no better at summarizing the effect of Dana's work as a librarian than to quote from an editorial in *The New York Sun*, appearing a few years before his death:

It's a dull day in Newark, N. J. on which John Cotton Dana does not find a new way to make the public library more useful. . . . If Newark's population does not attain intellectual supremacy over all the other people in the United States, its failure cannot fairly be laid at the door of the public library where Dana holds forth.

Whether he could lay claim to having made his city the most literate of all cities may well be doubted; but there can be no hesitation in according him the honor of making it more conscious of the resources in books than even its fondest friends would once have thought it could be. If I were skilful enough to draw a cartoon to illustrate what he was doing I should picture him leaning out of his office window beckoning with his finger and shouting an invitation to the people on the sidewalk to come in and see the treasures prepared for them. His achievement was not so much that he multiplied the number of borrowers or introduced a children's room or put on timely exhibits as that he galvanized the whole institution with his own living spirit. The place came to life under his hands. The staff loved it. People for whom experience was a dull round came to it to find release and hope. It was expansive and its lines ran out into all corners of the city. It was the workshop of an eager man and the glow of his enthusiasm was a light that kindled answering flames in the hearts of those whom it touched.

CHAPTER VIII

THE NEWARK MUSEUM

IN his youth Dana must often have gone to the country fairs. They were probably the most colorful events that he knew. Interested as he was in all the life that moved about him he undoubtedly wandered for hours inspecting the displays of produce, handwork, and livestock, each bearing the name of the farmer or community which had sent it, many of those names being as familiar to him as his own. The excitement of mingling with the crowds and tasting the special treats probably stamped upon his mind impressions he never forgot. These country fairs have a vitality of their own. Allowing for incidental changes in the character of the side-shows, they have maintained their peculiar flavor through all the years. Were a visitor of two generations ago to rise from his grave and re-visit a fair, he would find the main exhibits and programs much as he had familiarly known them.

One or two characteristics are worth mentioning. These annual fiestas are of the soil itself. They are incurably American and each one is colored and conformed by the indigenous life of the countryside. The people who attend are interested in what they see because it is the very stuff of their own lives. An unusual display of potatoes or of honey is their own workaday life lifted to excellence. An unusually effective snowplow attracts them because it is their own tool. Much of the appeal of what is exhibited lies in the arrangement achieved to make commonplace objects display their maximum beauty. There is sheer delight in seeing carrots and greens so juxtaposed as to make a picture pleasing to the eye. An event of beauty is made out of what is at hand. The whole constitutes an exhibition of skill that is entirely free from the exotic. The quilts, crochet and laces are patterns designed in native homes yet carrying the authentic touch of good workmanship approaching artistry. The colorful diversity of these displays redolent of the native soil must have stamped his mind with its validity, for he carried its pattern over into his conception of a museum. He definitely envisioned a museum as a place where actual life reported, where native skills were displayed, where exhibits were varied and changed periodically, and where nothing was shown merely because it was ancient, but only because it had authentic power to open men's eyes to the movement and meaning of the stream of life.

Newark had no museum when he came so he was able to develop one to his own taste. He began by opening a science museum on the fourth floor of the Library on February 25, 1905. In it he presented characteristic products of the city and models illuminating the scientific developments of the period. It was a thoroughly practical proposition, entirely divorced from any approach to either pretense or pretentiousness. In 1908 he secured the loan of the beautiful Rockwell collection of Japanese art objects and put them on display. They aroused a keen interest in the city upon which he capitalized to the extent of persuading the Mayor and Council to consider purchasing them. The result was a special law authorizing the city to buy them and to entrust them to a corporation formed for the purpose, to be known as the Newark Museum Association. Thus was formed on April 29, 1909 the Newark Museum with power to receive and administer whatever collections should be turned over to it.

Dana defined his museum work on the same premise as that of the library. It was to be no exploitation of the esoteric, but effort directed at affecting the masses of the people. He said that it was a mistake to build in "the style of a

local palace or royal residence" or to have "the art museum building set apart from the city proper." A municipality "can much better afford to move its museum into
the centers of daily movement of population and thereby
secure a tenfold enlargement of its use and influence." In
its early years, however, the problem of location did not
arise for the Newark Museum. It was housed in the building of the Public Library. Dana meanwhile acted as secretary of the Museum Association. On January 25, 1913, the
Association created the office of Director and elected him
to it. He was authorized to spend $500 a year in its man-
agement. By this time the organization had grown to the
point where it could report receipts of $19,550 and dis-
bursements of $11,700.

An article on "Live Museums" published the same year
reveals Dana restating his fundamental conviction. "Painting in oil upon canvas is not a craft that makes a strong appeal to the average man. . . . The fact that the oil painting
has no such close relation to the development of good taste
and refinement as have countless objects of daily use will
in time be recognized and acted upon. . . . If oil paintings
are put in the subordinate place in which they belong, the
average art museum will have much more room for the
display of objects which have quite a direct bearing on
the daily lives of those who support and visit it. . . . As the
museum gives more space and attention to these things it
will quite inevitably display the objects in which its own
city is particularly interested. It will have no absurd fear
that it will be commercialized and debased if it shows what
is being done to-day in the field of applied art in its own
city and in other parts of the world." In line with this general position he became a vigorous advocate of the encouragement of native contemporary artists through purchase
of their works. Writing to John Alexander and Joseph Pen-

nell, he declared: "My real purpose in writing you is to call your attention to the fact that New York has a huge building devoted to the promotion of art interests of all kinds. It is called the Metropolitan Museum of Art. This museum it is, with its vast plant, its huge endowment, and its liberal appropriations from the city, which should furnish rooms for the display of the American art of to-day of all kinds. . . . I look upon it as a piece of idle folly on the part of that institution that they decline not simply to buy, but, what is far more reprehensible, even to display the work of contemporary artists and artisans in any field." Thus Dana went on record as the pioneer among museum directors encouraging American art. He consistently displayed the work of contemporary artists, and established the precedent which has had its fruit in the growing interest in our native art and its development which now has such general support among museums, critics, patrons and the general public. He stated his position at length in 1914 in his book *American Art; How It Can Be Made To Flourish*.

Naturally, his criticism of the Metropolitan Museum at this one point did not mean any lack of appreciation on his part for the general excellence of its total program. In fact, he wrote a letter to the *New York Post* of April 17, 1918, expressing his admiration for it: "This letter serves its purpose if it calls attention to the supreme importance to this country of the Metropolitan Museum's store of treasures and to the fact that those who hold it in trust have so obviously gone beyond the conventional trusteeship idea, and have kept it for half a century, active, living, growing, and, to possible benefactors, a grateful civic organism." His interest in its work was not only keen, but warm, for his friend Henry W. Kent was now its secretary, having assumed that office in 1913, after nine years as assistant secretary. Mr. Kent, still happily alive and active, was a collaborator with Mr. Dana in many enterprises, and always a valiant supporter of his ideals.

In 1916 Newark celebrated its 250th anniversary. The original plans for this celebration included the erection of a Memorial Building. Since it was proposed that the Museum be located in it, Mr. Dana was actively interested in all the discussions and decisions relating to it. He prepared a lengthy account of how he visualized the building as a central place for large civic gatherings of all kinds and for exhibits displaying the varied phases of general effort and local interest. Characteristically he laid his first emphasis on its being in a location close to the center of the city. It was on precisely this point that a sharp difference of opinion arose between him and the majority of the committee, so that he and Charles Bradley resigned. It seems that a small group within the committee took matters in their own hands and selected a site, somewhat removed from the center of the city, without having given any consideration to the kind of building to be erected. When this action was reported as a final decision Dana wrote a sharp, uncompromising denunciation of it. The *Newark News* took up the battle and, in an editorial of January 3, 1916, pointed out that the property selected involved pieces of land in which three members of the committee were interested either personally or through the institutions they controlled. On the day this editorial appeared, Wallace M. Scudder, publisher of the paper, resigned from the committee. By this time the city was aroused. One prominent member of the committee practically insulted Dana in a public place, and, as one correspondent put it, "In Newark there exists a state of civil strife." The Memorial Committee decided to ask the opinion of the citizens on the whole issue. The outcome was that no building was erected, and Dana continued to administer the museum in the Library Building. His courage had prevented a doubtful use of $1,500,000 of public funds, and his determination had kept the museum from being exiled to a spot then comparatively far from the places where people naturally met.

Speaking before the American Association of Museums in May of this same year, Dana emphasized "Increasing the Usefulness of Museums."

It is easy for a museum to get objects; it is hard for a museum to get brains. . . . Probably no more useless public institution was ever devised than that popular ideal, the classical building of a museum of art, filled with rare and costly objects. . . . To its community it gives a specious promise of artistic regeneration, and it permits those who visit it to put on certain integuments of culture which, although they do not conceal esthetic nakedness, inhibit the free exercise of both intellect and sensibility. . . . If, now, museums are to be of great use to the world, here are the things that museum brains must fight against: fashionable museum buildings, fashionable museum collections, and fashionable treatment of collections. . . . A museum is good only in so far as it is of use. . . . Common sense demands that a publicly supported institution do something for its supporters, and that some part at least of what it does be capable of clear description and downright valuation. . . .

He goes on to describe his idea of a real museum, as if it were actually in existence:

The Museum is near the center of the daily movement of its citizens. . . . The halls of wonders contain a few examples of the oil paintings, sculptures, and curios which every museum of art is supposed to possess, and a few of the habitat groups, large skeletons, and curiosities of nature which convention bids us look for in a museum of science. If these were not on view in a convenient place and near the entrance, they would be earnestly and persistently sought by visitors until they were found. By putting them near the entrance and by giving the entrance just a touch of grandeur, all visitors who have the conventional museum expectancy enjoy at once the agreeable reactions they look for, and are fit to proceed further with a quiet and receptive mind. . . .

Our projected institute contains the following:

1. A staff adequate for the work which the objects named and the activities suggested may require. The staff is larger, relatively to size of building and cost of collections, and more highly paid, than it is in any existing museum of equal floor-space.

2. Paintings, chiefly recent American, but with an abundance of copies of old masterpieces . . . some are lent to schools, some are placed in windows of stores. . . .

3. Sculptures, including many American bronzes and others of all countries and all times, the latter being in most cases inexpensive copies. Most of these are usually stored, or lent, or are on exhibition in other places. . . .

4. Prints, a large collection . . .

5. A collection of about a million pictures of paintings, sculptures, architecture, and chiefly, of decorated objects of daily use. . . . These are used by students in the building and are lent freely. . . .

6. Collections of metal and woodwork, textiles, etc.

7. A selection, constantly changing through rejections and renewals, of things made in the city. Of some of these an important exhibit is held each year. . . .

8. Many objects illustrating such fundamental industries, whether followed in the city or not, as have greatly influenced the development of civilization: objects of clay and glass, textiles, leather, metal objects, jewelry, wood and foods.

9. Habitat groups.

10. Science collections.

11. A library, for reference and lending use.

12. Lanterns, lantern-slides, stereomotorgraphs, moving picture films . . .

13. A department of cooperation.

14. With this department goes another which gives its times chiefly to instructing teachers and others in the art of visual instruction. . . .

15. Workshops.

16. Branches.

17. A school.

That he was able to make his projection of the ideal museum a fact in practice is indicated by the report of Arséne Alexandre, sent by the French government to study in America the reorganization of art instruction following the war. He picked the Newark Museum as "a model of good sense and originality." Le Comité Central Technique des Arts Appliqués gave special study to the museum as a result of these findings.

As in the case of the Library, Dana worked for a close alliance between the Museum and the public schools. He designed exhibits that could be taken to the schools and displayed in them. He also cooperated with teachers by having on exhibition at the Museum itself objects illustrating their classroom work. The result was regular visits by classes of children under the supervision of their teachers and with members of the Museum staff acting as docents. One of the most affecting sights of Newark to-day is a class of these children marshalled in pairs on their way to visit a display especially set up to catch their imaginations.

Alongside this activity closely related to school programs, there grew up the Junior Museum. In it on Saturday mornings children met to model, paint, fashion, study, create and print as their desires dictated. The stories of those who found here the beginnings of interests which have become their professions are worthy of a book in themselves. One young man has grown into an expert on the snakes of New Jersey, another is now engaged in archeological research, and several have turned their minds to various crafts. The Junior Museum has flourished particularly under the friendly eyes of Beatrice Winser who, in the Museum also, added her gifts to those of Mr. Dana to help make his work complete.

One of his standing rules for the institution was that no exhibit should remain on display too long. He had no hesitation about relegating objects to the storeroom temporarily. He insisted on variety. It was here that his originality made itself felt. At one time, he put on a display of modern plumbing conveniences as an expression of his firm conviction that contemporary craftsmanship was achieving its own kind of beauty. At another time he exhibited pottery. As the visitors passed through, they greeted the graceful lines with suitably appreciative "Ah's" and "Oh's." When they reached the end, they found a neatly typewritten sign: "All the objects in this collection were bought in the local five and ten cent stores, no single object costing more than twenty-five cents."

He balanced this kind of immediate interest with exhibits leading to interpretations of wider areas, thus balancing the provincial with the cosmopolitan. For example, in recognition of the growing importance of South America, as early as 1918 he displayed pictures and objects showing the people, resources, business conditions, exports, imports and exporting methods of Colombia. President Wilson sent him a note of congratulation on this exhibit, and later it was taken to the Bush Terminal Building in New York City. It was characteristic of Dana that he did not go into New York for the opening, but sent a letter instead.

Always he was working, talking and writing for a live museum. In Newark he confronted indifference and no small antagonism. In the museum world he met the same attitudes. He did not bow to these influences. In fact, he probably enjoyed his museum work all the more because the conventions were against him. Sometimes a critic of his work would find some minor inaccuracy in a catalogue or a date, and, pouncing on it, would magnify it out of all proportion, practically discrediting a whole display with this incidental flaw. Dana knew how to meet such. He was clear in his own mind about what he was trying to do. He was interpreting the use of things, not the facts about them, and he could take an error in his stride if the main purpose were served.

Following the custom he had maintained in his library work, Dana organized in 1925 an apprentice class in museum work. Applicants sought admission to these annual classes from all over the country. He carefully selected from six to eight college graduates each year, and gave them training in his methods over a period of nine months. In the course he included six weeks of intensive work in the Newark Public Library, and each student was required to undertake a small piece of printing. More than seventy-five young people have passed through these classes, and many of them are now employed in museums throughout the country.

The problem of housing the Museum Association's objects in the Library grew more and more pressing, so that in 1922 the City Commissioners voted to purchase land for a Museum Building. In accordance with Dana's ideas, the site selected was close to the center of the city, being the old Marcus L. Ward homestead on Washington Street close to the Public Library and facing Washington Park. On the Board of the Museum sat Louis Bamberger, Newark's most successful merchant, a quiet man who watched Dana's work with keen and appreciative eyes. In 1923 he came forward with the offer to give to the city a Museum Building. Jarvis Hunt was chosen as the architect. For many months Bamberger, Hunt and Dana worked over the plans, finally designing a three story building, planned around a central court, and having a limestone façade. They avoided the pitfalls of the conventional and the merely decorative and produced a practical edifice adapted to many uses. The building and its equipment cost $750,-000. It was formally opened on March 17, 1926. At the rear of this building is a large walled garden and Dana planted this so as to make of it both a place of rest for visitors and a display of growing things. Beds of flowers change with the seasons. A Shakespeare garden contains the plants mentioned by the poet. Pieces of sculpture, ancient and modern, are advantageously placed. A clump of willows shadow a bird bath, and varieties of trees and shrubs are cultivated.

The new building stimulated gifts. Especially pleasing, in view of Dana's pioneer work, was a collection of contemporary paintings and American sculpture, given by Mr. Bamberger's sister, Mrs. Felix Fuld, and her husband, Felix Fuld. The selection of the individual pieces was largely made by Arthur F. Egner, a lawyer, who had caught Dana's enthusiasm and who was afterwards to become president of the Museum, and Holger Cahill and the artists themselves. Such gifts as this posed new problems to the director, but assisted by Beatrice Winser and his staff, he found new joy in them. When questioned by a reporter on his work, his almost boyish comment was: "I've had a lot of fun. A whole lot of fun!" Then, moving into a more serious mood, he said:

The museum is, I believe, all right, though I shall have to admit that now the building is completed and the museum moved into it, I find myself at the end of my immediate imagination. I am going ahead as fast as money permits, but I discover that I am more and more of the opinion I have held for years, that nobody knows how to run a museum.

CHAPTER IX

HIS MIND AND THE ARTS

SOME day a wise man and scholar will trace the influence of granite on brains. There seems to be a definite relationship between the apparent inhospitality of the mountains and the independence of mind of those who live among them. The English have never been able to absorb the Scots for the men north of the Tweed have a mental tenacity that defies all the smooth beguilings of intellectual compromise. Every Scot knows that he is mentally superior to the Sassenach, and that if he is not actually wealthier and more powerful it is only because he has not taken the trouble to go to London to be elected president of a corporation or to be made Prime Minister. In areas where brains count, in theology or philosophy or learning, he is proudly sure that Scotland leads the Empire. And we cannot laugh too loudly at him, for he can probably prove his case. He is a man of independent mind springing from a soil where every child is nurtured in high thinking and every home is the anteroom to a university.

Vermont is the Scotland of the United States. The Vermonter knows his own mind, and even though other states and even the Federal Government may go dancing after purple dreams of unprecedented social panaceas he walks his own gait and finds no particular embarrassment in his solitude. He insists on listening to reason and speaking his own mind. To him, at least, it was no surprise that when an extravagant and orgiastic national administration had to be cleaned up on the death of its leader, a Vermont boy was the one for the job. Others might wonder or even scoff at the curiously un-American silences of Calvin Coolidge but every Vermonter understood a man who kept quiet

unless he had something to say. You cannot argue a rocky
field into giving you a crop, you just have to keep your
mouth shut and dig the rocks out. The bleak and reverent
beauty of Vermont makes philosophers of all its sons. They
think. This may be because they have so much of solitari-
ness, and it may be the reason they seem quaint to the rest
of us, but the fact remains, they think. You do not know a
Vermonter until you see how his mind works.

All of Dana's accomplishments grew out of his philosophy of life and work. This may sound trite, but it is worth
emphasizing because his philosophy was conscious and articulate. He knew where he was and where he wanted to
go and had a clear idea of the road he intended to take.
As a member of the relatively rational human race he
lived by patterns of behavior designed to an unusual degree
by his own rational understanding of himself. His mind
charted the course of his conduct.

It is characteristic of him that he approached his philosophy of art through the work of the printers. He writes
of "the most democratic of art's mediums of expression—
the printing-press." He himself loved books and he knew
that nearly every person in our American community reads
something. Many may read no more than the newspapers,
but he took that into account, insisting that the contents
of these have to be arranged, and that, therefore, they are
examples of form. "Let me suggest that even this most
democratic of the products of the printing press—the daily
paper—makes for the democratization of art. Almost every
page or almost every daily paper is carefully designed.
The persons who make up the several forms exercise all
the skill and taste they have in arranging the type in hand
for the next edition. But study and practice in design do
not begin in the make-up of the page. To the selection of
the type, the length and number of the lines, the space and

arrangement of all the headings in the paper, has gone much preliminary thought in which style, distinction, attractiveness and beauty were not ignored."

He could appreciate the achievements of the printer's art because all his life he was himself a printer. "Charlie Montague was the first man to lead me into printer's ink. He was the all around man in the *Vermont Standard* office right across Elm Street from my home. When he wet the paper, I stood by and admired and got my first sprinkling of typographic holy water from the wash basin and sprinkling broom, his complete moistening apparatus. Charlie it was who later told us boys how to get up our monthly paper, *The Acorn*, and I still claim no better looking journal ever jumped into the amateur arena. . . . Later days in Denver brought me to Harry Carson who showed me how a library's printing could have something besides legibility. . . . In Springfield a dear old printer translated my vague desires for good printing into beauties that cling to me yet. . . . Then in Newark came to me an inspired salesman. He sold me an ancient Washington press and cleancut notions of typography. So, quite late in life, with two fonts of type, a hand press and a brayer, I carried on as a library near-printer. I have looked with awe upon Mr. Updike and Mr. Bruce Rogers."

The standards which he applied to printing were simplicity, taste, and skill in workmanship. "Anything intended to be read that is less of legibility than the maximum that can be attained is wrong; and if in suppressing legibility the designer of a piece of printing thinks he is doing something for art, then I can assure you he is entirely mistaken." He felt that a pitfall of American printing was its attempt to do too much, to overload with ornamentation that fails to square with true artistic standards. The form that serves maximum utility is the purest and, to that extent, the most artistic. "If knowledge is a good thing for us to have, then a method of making it easier to acquire is not to be dismissed off-hand."

He gave practical expression to his love of the art of printing. The Newark Public Library collected examples of modern commercial printing and organized a comprehensive reference file of its varied collection of printers' products. In 1904 a first exhibition was organized, and in 1908 a larger one enriched by carefully acquired treasures including manuscripts written before the invention of printing, examples of early bookprinting, specimens of old and famous presses, volumes from the finest contemporary printers, and histories of the art of printing. During subsequent years Dana organized these exhibits of the art of the printers in many ways, sometimes displaying the work of many of the masters of the craft, and sometimes showing one man's work. His efforts not only stimulated the interest of the general public, but stirred the enthusiasm of professional printers. Henry Lewis Bullen wrote in 1918: "The showing of the complete works of Bruce Rogers might well serve as a model of what exhibits of printing should be, and confirmed and vivified every ideal of the printers who saw it. Something must be done to stimulate scholarship and art among receptive, studious printers all over this country, and Dana has made a beginning. Let the scholarly printers journey to Newark and gain inspiration from him: not a mere librarian as custodian of books, but a dispenser of light and knowledge, and an apostle of the finer things of life."

He not only displayed the excellent printing of others but he planned the publications of his own institutions with an eye for their value as examples of good craftsmanship. The principle behind this he stated explicitly: "Through its printing every library reaches its public in a most intimate way, and by it can do much to improve the taste of the public in one of the most important of all the industrial arts." He was quick to appreciate examples of good printing produced by all institutions. For example, in 1909 he wrote to the *New York Evening Post* praising the catalogue of the Hudson-Fulton exhibition at the Metropolitan Museum, calling attention to its value as a contribution to the history of the arts crafts in America, and giving especial mention to its form and typographic style.

He and his brothers operated a press of their own in the old store at Woodstock. It is still in existence and is carrying the name they gave it, The Elm Tree Press. Henry W. Kent has described it: "This press is intimately identified with the welfare and all the best activities of the place where it is located, Woodstock, Vermont. Here four of Woodstock's sons, members of one family intimately associated with the village since its earliest decade, proud of its record and infused with its spirit—Medicus Bibliophile and Bibliothecar noted in cities far from their home town, and Bibliograph and Typographer—have set up the Elm Tree Press. It is the spirit which they infused into their types that makes the individuality of their accomplishment, a spirit which unites love of human interests, politics, village life, golf, the classics, wit which stands as one of the fundamentals, and, of course, love of the Fathers of Typography."

Dana's love of printing and approach to artistic appreciation through it has something of the Athenian about it. He did not come to "Art" with a capital "A," he came to artisanship and found art in its apotheosis. Because he had known the agony of making up a page, of having to amplify and cut down words to fill space, of choosing type to suit matter, and of printer's ink on his fingers, he could appreciate the skill and balance of a well printed page. In

1911 Harvard University invited seventeen lecturers to
appear in a course on "An Introduction to the Technique
of Printing." Mr. Dana was one of them and the outline
of his lecture is a series of steps that summarize his own
development in the understanding of the printer's work:
(i) the importance of printing and allied trades in modern
industry; (ii) the influence of printing on progress in general and especially on progress in civility and refinement;
(iii) the growth of esteem and respect for the trade of printing; (iv) the revival of appreciation of the printer as a designer; (v) the printer as a creator, and the pleasures of his
calling. The utilitarian premise blossomed gradually into
the flowering art. In another place he put the same thought
in another way: "Getting things done is to everyone more
important than getting them beautifully done. . . . But
there are a few who print well because they must and they
help a little. . . . Our problem is to find a few boys who
are willing to be taught what good printing really is. . . .
Printers cannot sell beautiful printing until the buyers of
printing recognize what good printing is."

In his mind what he called "good printing" was an admirable introduction to esthetic emotions. "Now, print is
to-day about the most common of all the human-made objects that meet our eyes. We easily learn to read it, that is,
it is merely legible almost by nature. But it can be infi-
nitely more. If you take a little time to compare merely
legible printing with genuinely good printing, and thus
gain the ability to see even vaguely the essential difference
between them, then you will add to your other possibilities of pleasant emotions."

From the page of print to the printed picture is a natural step. Dana took it boldly. He made no apologies for
seeing the drawings and pictures of the newspapers as introductions to the whole field of understanding of the work

of pictorial artists. "The illustrations in the daily papers are not to be dismissed with simply a word of condemnation. They have come and are here to stay. They are often useful and frequently entertaining. They are in many cases so bad that to call them pictures is an insult to the word, and they are in many cases employed to make a disgraceful, degrading and disgusting story more disgraceful, degrading and disgusting still. But the bad art and bad morals of newspaper illustration are only incidents in the wonderful development of a powerful educational tool. Much that is worth reading may be read in pictures, or with their aid, in a fraction of the time it takes to read it in print." He maintained that the picture in black and white may be full of delicate suggestions of harmonies of line and shade and of skill in arrangement to those who look upon them as works of art. Of all the beautiful things which surround us and appeal to us for recognition and appreciation every day, one of the commonest, easiest to understand, least expensive to acquire and most fundamental in its teaching is the study in black and white.

He even tilted a lance for the funny papers. His answer to their critics was: "Understand why they exist. Examine the conditions that produce them. Lend a hand at improving the conditions, and so improve the product." He did not stop at this, however. He declared that humorous illustrations are products of a movement that is helpful in the growth of interest in art and in the development of draftsmen, designers and colorists. This declaration was not an attempt at sensationalism, nor was it a concession to mediocrity. It came out of a conviction that native art must find its own forms and feed on whatever nourishment the native culture chooses to provide. He once stated this point of view with incisiveness: "I am finding fault with the opinion I myself held, gathered from very general reading, that the Renaissance of Italy was something different from the development of art and letters now going on in Omaha, Chicago and Hoboken. And it is no shame to say that if more and better works were asked for from them, with greater rewards of cash, opportunity and esteem, more good artists would be forthcoming and an American Renaissance would begin."

This emphasis on encouragement of local expression as an exciting impetus to real growth of contemporary art made him a vigorous critic of those who worshipped "these art fellows" of other times, but overlooked the striving efforts of their own living fellows. In an article written in 1916 on "Questions about American Art" he put a blunt question:

In Cleveland, Ohio, was recently opened an art museum. I examined the catalogue with care and in it found that the articles and pictures described were not, with a very few exceptions, made in Cleveland or in this country, and that they did not bear any direct relation to the daily life or the daily activities of anyone in Cleveland. Why not? In New York is published a journal called *Art in America*. It is not concerned with art in America at all. Is this journal called *Art in America* because its promoters believe that there is no art in America except that which the rich have brought here?

In a recent number of *Art and Archeology* is an article on art in Buffalo. It describes the building of the Albright Art Gallery and tells of the development of the collections in that gallery and of the activities which led to its erection. It says nothing whatever of art in Buffalo. About this I repeat the question I asked concerning Cleveland.

Can you give me the answer?

He was not in all this giving expression to a kind of artistic patriotism. The important fact in his mind was not that a given piece of work should be American, but that the American community should be the kind of environment compatible to genius, so that we should produce beauty in our own forms rather than rest content to house the survivals of other men's dreaming and achievement. He once said: "Beauty has no relation to price, rarity or age."

To this Henry W. Kent replied: "Is there then no fittest? Since you don't admit that price, rarity or age has anything to do with Beauty you destroy the nice old tradition of the survival of the fittest, and, along with it, Hellas!"

Dana answered: "Fitness is not bought with a price,—it survives; surviving it becomes common, not rare;—and time ripens the essence of its fitness, not by giving it age, but by daily making it in some aspect new."

Life proves its vitality by its ability to be contemporary, to go on in the world of to-day, and while the memory of departed men may serve to spur their survivers, these latter will not long survive if they remember and do no more. So Beauty becomes an esoteric cult if it be not a present experience. Dana could admire his Tintoretto with any man, but medieval Venice producing such a man was to him but a promise of modern Newark begetting such another and stamping him with her authentic seal.

The point he continually made was that any community and any country gets the kind of art that it deserves. And art demands good seers as well as good painters. What do people who look at pictures see? Here is his answer: "We may describe the picture-gazing of the average person somewhat as follows: he likes the color; he likes to look because others look; he likes to look because he enjoys seeing an old friend; because he has the habit of looking; because he enjoys seeing the curious; because he enjoys the sympathy with his fellows which comes from enjoying the same objects with them; because he enjoys the story of the picture; because the picture renews for him an incident in history; because considered simply as a design the picture is to his thinking well made and he finds agreeable the relation of its lines and its colors and their arrangement, their harmonies and their contrasts; and because, having skill as a painter or knowing of that skill, he is interested in the manner in which the artist in question laid on his paint."

He stressed the art of appreciating art by giving an individual touch to the introductions he wrote for the catalogues of his exhibitions. When he presented a display of water-colors, for example, he brought out the distinctive qualities to observe:

To those who are not familiar with modern water colors, especially the products of American artists of latter years, this exhibition will be something of a surprise. The English have long prided themselves on their supremacy in this particular form of art. Their method has been and still is quite strongly ruled by certain conventions. Water-colors in the English understanding, as one writer says, to be consistent must be wet, and the picture which does not show very distinctly that the colors on it were floated on with an abundance of water is not considered as properly a water-color. The Americans have not held fast to these conventions. They have not hesitated to use an abundance of paint when an abundance of paint put on in any way they saw fit produced a result they sought. The American water-colors are, from the English point of view, not always legitimate or proper. That is, the colors used in them are not always transparent, but, as an English critic says, the American, if he wishes to get an effect in water-color by means of body color, tries it and often succeeds. Another English authority says that water-color art as practiced in America is fresh and vital, and has a distinctly national note.

He seized eagerly on every opportunity to stir groups to active participation in creating a public demand for art. His theory was that talent emerges in response to sympathetic or even critical understanding in the social environment. Phidias produced his masterpieces because the people

of Athens were in love with Beauty, and in their insistence on excellence he found both the incentive and the
reward of his effort. Genius is an individual gift, but its
culture is a social achievement. If there are enough people who want the superlative badly enough someone will
emerge to produce it for them. In this sense, genius is a
social product. So Dana tried to cultivate members of all
sorts of groups as units of artistic expectation, feeling that
American art will emerge in an environment suffused with
enthusiasm for it. As he told the Woman's Club of Orange
on one occasion:

The sum of it is: America produces few objects of art because it is
too busy to appreciate them.

To learn to know and feel beauty in everyday objects produced
in America, this is to study American art.

In art matters it is more important to be sensitive than to be
knowing. It is better worth while to feel that a thing is right and
to get pleasure from that feeling, than it is to know who made it,
when and where and under what conditions, who has owned it and
who now owns it and what he paid for it. If you cultivate your
sensibilities by the keen observation and careful criticism of every-
day familiar objects, you cultivate thereby the whole esthetic side
of your nature.

Study your tea-cups. A fascinating study would be the door
knocker. Study printing and the printed book.

He could not resist a specific application of his exhortation:

Do you think that, as students and friends of art and the art crafts,
you live up to the most modest of aspirations when you join in the
production of a Federation Year Book like that of 1909–10? I am
not criticizing the printer; he gave you all you paid for and I pre-
sume a little more. But in this product you, banded together to
make life within our State broader and finer and more joyful, have
permitted yourselves to go on record as favoring the cheap and the
commonplace.

In a similar vein he brought his lesson home to the Eastern Art Teachers Association: "I have tried to intimate that American Life is essentially laborious, productive, money-getting; that the people consequently think a little and work much, and, like all hard workers among crops either of gold or potatoes, are not quick or nice in their emotions. They wish their colors strong, their stories crude and their humor broad. They think the picture good if it cost much, the statue if it make much talk. They are keen on esthetics when convention says to them they should be; but then only." Again came the irresistible impulse to administer a sly dig: "Why, some of your members trip daily past the dishevelled ash box and the fragrant garbage can, and move on swiftly to teach the children how to spot and how to spatter by the laws of balance, harmony and rhythm,—like the rest of us, esthetic only at an appointed time and place." He closed on the serious note:

My conclusion is that, if you wish to hasten the day when there shall be some relation between Art and Life in America, you must, as far as your work is concerned, make sure that it does something other than give a little more skill to those who are born skilful; that it breed, by exposure and suggestion and practice, the habit of having feelings about all that they see.

As for what constitutes Beauty, he was of the opinion that every man must find his own answer. "Why do we think that a row of Greek columns is beautiful? The attempt to answer this question has brought me to the conclusion that there are no standards of beauty and no principles in art or universal application; that there is no definable esthetic field; that every man finds certain things beautiful because of the character of his own body and mind; and that every man, therefore, has within himself a standard of beauty for himself alone, and can discover no other."

When Mr. Jenkinson asked him for advice about understanding and appreciating art he wrote him:

Whatever gives a man pleasure when he looks at it is, by the very nature of things, to him a work of art and the pleasure he gets from it is esthetic.

All this talk about different degrees of art, and art principles, and the laws for making beautiful things, is nonsense except for the man who makes them! The next man must make his own. There are no principles in art save those which every man has for himself, and they are due to the kind of body, brain, eyes and education that he himself has.

Men have made some things, like the Parthenon, which other men have admired for several hundred years. The savage would not admire them. The time will come when the cultured European will not think much of them. I mean we will outgrow things like the Parthenon. We will have different notions about what architecture should be.

This kind of an approach to artistic standards grew out of his preoccupation always with the wonder of individuality. He began with the unique fact, and left to others the inclusive generalizations. Any law, as a description of living behavior, is an attempt to state the characteristics of the average; examined closely enough each individual varies somewhat from the norm, that is, is an exception to the rule. One type of mind concentrates on the areas that events have in common, another is attracted by individual variations. Dana's was of the second type. He specialized by temperament in the concrete.

For example, when he was talking about the use of flowers in education he insisted: "The purpose is not to use flowers as a means of decoration, but to bring out the beauty of flower, branch, fruit, or of the whole plant; to call attention to the individuality of stem, leaf, bloom and fruit." He was always calling attention to individuality, finding his satisfactions not in the standardized but in the unique. He believed that men and events are all interesting at their points of abnormality rather than of compliance. This simply means that he was essentially a man of sceptical mind. He would have made a good Athenian but an irritating monk.

Artistically, however, he found his major satisfaction in the work of the Japanese. This is not strange. Writing is consciously an art in Japan where every man works with his fine brush to create beautiful characters. In such a setting it is natural that all art should be a kind of writing. The written letter is the most economical of all symbols and, though standardized in itself, can be combined with other letters in multiplied and eloquent forms. All Japanese art takes on some of writing's characteristics. Its effects are produced with maximum economy of line; and although its forms are so conventional as to appear stilted at first glance they are worked together so subtly and ingeniously that they surprise and excite the trained eye. Simplicity, arrangement and skill in workmanship are all present, and these to Dana were the evidences of high art.

He collected all forms of Japanese art himself and secured valuable objects for the Museum. The prints were his especial delight, and he became an expert in deciphering the baffling signatures of the artists. Among these artists his especial favorite was Hiroshige. And of all Hiroshige he loved best "The Black Bridge," to which he wrote the following lines:

Giant posts march in ranks
Across the mighty flood . . .
. . . Above, the vast grey waste of sky.
Below the gently shimmering waters,
Of blueness inconceivable, yet true!

A tender cloud of birds
Above the bridge intensifies
The thought that this, indeed,
Is Air, is Air!

Upon the stream the boats
Weave in and out amid the mighty posts
And pass from here to there,
From there to here,
And mark, as conquered,
Th' unconquerable flood.
Beyond, across the stream,
Far, far beyond,
A black and serried rank
Of homes of those whose ships
Have conquered the wide stream,
Of those whose power and skill
Have spanned the blue, blue flood.

And on the bridge, forever,
Above the indomitable waters,
High in the pregnant air
Safe on a thousand sturdy posts
Goes endlessly to and fro
The flood of humanity.
Here pass in safety to
Their distant homes,
The genii of the bridge
And of the ships. . . .

. . . . Perchance among them the dreamer
He of the eye impeccable,
The creator and the seer
Himself, Hiroshige!

CHAPTER X

BOOKS, EDUCATION, POLITICS, AND SOCIETY

ARISTOTLE came close to a universal human predilection when he started the business of classifying the phenomena of the universe. Most of us have an urge to turn our minds into filing cabinets with every drawer carefully marked, its contents tidily arranged, providing us with a place for everything, so that we can keep everything in its place. I used to have a professor who could outline the universe on a blackboard. But I could never get over the feeling of relief when he took an eraser and rubbed the outline out. It was as if he gave the universe back to us then. The empty board was so ponderable a symbol of all that had escaped the busy piece of chalk.

Classifying all other events, it is natural that philosophers have classified themselves. So every member of the fraternity becomes a something-ist. To trace the devious windings of a complex mind wrestling with the mystery of experience becomes unnecessary when all you have to do is to "place" him. Why bother to read a man when you already know he is an ideal-ist, or a pragmat-ist, or a pessim-ist, or an instrumental-ist? Undoubtedly we have to classify to organize our thinking, but that does not mean that we must suspend all intellectual effort except that of memorizing our categories. A man has to be able to do more than arrange words in alphabetical order even to be a lexicographer; and it is the man who ignores the alphabetical order who writes Don Juan. The precise critics on *The Edinburgh Review* knew that Byron was not writing poetry by the careful and classified rules; they were erudite and exact; they knew everything, in fact, except the one thing that mattered, namely, that Byron was a poet.

Dana insisted in all matters that intellectual pride easily clothes itself in pompous pretence and sometimes cloaks itself so thoroughly that it covers its own eyes and is none the less blind for being arrogant. He held that every man is a sovereign fact in his own right and has the inherent privilege of looking out on the world through his own window. In a world of echoes he listened for the living voices.

When he sat down to write a speech to teachers on the use of books he put his whole philosophy of reading into twelve rules:

1. Read
2. Read
3. Read some more
4. Read anything
5. Read about everything
6. Read enjoyable things
7. Read things you yourself enjoy
8. Read, and talk about it
9. Read very carefully—some things
10. Read on the run, most things
11. Don't think about reading, but
12. Just read.

Behind these rules was his faith in the capacity of the mind to discover its own nutrition through its natural hungers even though these make it a wanderer in many fields. It is a faith justified of many of its children, though a case may be made for a lesser licence to discursiveness. Ulysses travelled in many lands and was all the more Ulysses for his varied exploits, but Penelope kept a kind of integrity by staying faithfully at home. At any rate, Dana was on the side of Ulysses:

I don't like to use the word, but it is true that to be cultivated you must be superficial. There are only two or three things at best that any of you can know, know well and intimately. You can get culture by a combination of several methods. But the fundamental things in culture—which is superficial knowledge—and in pleasure, these can always be had in reading. Find something good in reading—good in your opinion—and have a good time with it. And keep eternally at it. If you keep on reading you find that the poison of one book has its antidote in another; that what you last year thought was charming you now find is silly; that your former dislikes now seem the prejudices of an ignoramus; and that where you thought you had only scraps of knowledge in your mind you now have, on some topic your reading has randomly touched a score of times, an ordered array of doctrine. The active mind digests rapidly and is always hungry. To feed it, read. Don't fear mental dyspepsia, but watch out for mental starvation.

In another place he put his position in a quotable sentence: "Books are well read by those who like to read them, not by those who feel they ought to read them; just as good deeds are well done by those who like to do them, not by those who fear not to do them, or those who hope by doing them to acquire merit."

Rabbi Stephen S. Wise once wrote him that his son, on going to a new school, had picked up reading habits of a distressing kind:—"Some boys have gotten at him and put in his way books about baseball victories, crew triumphs and football successes. As a result, he wishes to read nothing else but that sort of stuff. I turn to you as an expert to ask you what is the wisest plan to pursue. The boy's mother wants to forbid that sort of reading, but I am dubious as to the wisdom of that plan, thinking that within a few months that fever will wear itself out." Dana answered:

I have to make a confession first and say that I do not know what to answer, then I save my face by asserting that nobody else knows. But here are my guesses. The average boy can be guided in his reading by his parents and teachers and friends absolutely, and if the guiding is wise the boy will not be greatly disturbed or grieved by it. With most boys, however, this guiding will lead to some extent to the habit of being guided, which is, of course, not good for the boy. Am I not right in thinking that it is generally better to let a boy learn by experience than never to permit him to have the experience? Again a boy should live in his own times even while still a boy. He should in most cases wear the clothes, learn the lessons, play the games, read the papers and books, in harmony with the boys of his own age and country. . . . But, after all, I do not hesitate to give this advice: That you let the boy read some of nearly all the things that the boys he likes to play with are reading; that you see to it that he reads them openly; that he has the books at home on his own shelves; that you know about them yourself even to the extent of reading some of them. . . . If the boy has something of his father, the time will come when the remarks that you and his mother drop, from time to time, about the value of this or that, the silliness of this or that, the kind of men who have liked to get profit from this or that, and so on, will take effect.

He stood resolutely for the principle of personal selection in reading. "Good poetry to be good poetry must be good to him who reads it, if it is indeed good to its reader then it is indeed good poetry." In a playful mood he announced:

A club has just been formed to suppress Shakespearitis. The directors have authorized me to present an outline of the reasons for the formation of this society. Many persons read a little of Shakespeare and think they hereby become literary. They read him and think they are acquiring culture, when they are simply cultivating conceit of culture—which is one of the most injurious affections of the human mind. They read him and think they are getting wise when they are simply getting the pleasure of familiarity with platitudinous quotations. They read him and think they are studying human nature, while in fact they are merely learning the names of characters in plays. They read him and think they are studying morals and improving their own, while in fact they are simply echoing the same conventions which they swap with their neighbors over the back fence, and are growing smug in the thought that they are not as bad as Richard III. The function of this noble society of ours is to check this literary self-deception, this injurious conceit of culture.

He frankly expressed the opinion that much literary talk is mere pretense; that we learn in school about certain "great books" but read only a few of them; that we have every right not to read them if we do not really like them. In fact, he gave it as verdict that certain books may be great, vital and fundamental, containing within them much of light and power, and yet have a message for a small circle only. The classics of literature may not be everybody's business. He would rather win people to the habit of reading by letting them read what they find pleasurable than make reading a burden by trying to enforce literary imperatives. "Print may be the new factor which will save our civilization. It is of supreme importance, therefore, that we learn to read. At present we read little because the art is one for which our brains do not inherit the apparatus."

He praised novels because they captured people's interest and made readers out of them. He also saw in them the chance to educate the imagination to see men and events of kinds differing from those of the reader's own sphere of experience. With Frances D. Twombly he edited an anthology of *Scenes From Good Novels Depicting Joy In Work.* In the introduction he wrote: "To both of us it has seemed that many well-intentioned books, laboriously setting forth outlines of world industries do not give adequate impressions of these industries. Surely some can be found in descriptions of workshops written by writers of insight and imagination, like our novelists. In their hands many occupations seem as definitely to live as does the man who follows them, and even to have souls which, like the souls of the men themselves, are touched with romance."

At the dedication of the Trenton Library in 1902 he uttered a prophecy on the future of the novel, which some recent instances prove was not too bold: "You will lend from this library many novels. I believe in them. They are destined to play a part in our life in the next few decades. A few hundred thousand read them now; in a few years millions will read them. We are expressing ourselves through them; in them we are putting our history, our hopes, our ideals." Two decades later he could write what was almost a confirmation of his own forecast:

Almost all the men who work as if they liked it, who move quickly, who use their brains and have brains to use and who get things done, are fond of reading novels. I conclude from this that the story-teller has always had the attention of the wise men of his generation—just as he has their attention now. I also conclude that the writer of novels to-day is as little harmful and as greatly cheering and helpful to vigorous and competent workers to-day as was the story-teller in generations past.

The novel of to-day seems to express the present man more fully than any other form of literature. It can touch all subjects, express all feelings, teach all doctrines. Unless all signs fail, it is sure to widen its field still further, to become still more widely read, to teach us more readily, to set forth character, history, theories, ideas and doctrines more comprehensively still.

When he discussed the popularity of the novel among readers with Michael Randall in 1922, he declared:

Current novels are the eggs of the library business; nobody wants them when they are old! And, like eggs, they are called for principally by women. It would be interesting to know what classes of men read most the country over. Without being able to quote definite statistics I imagine that such a study would show that lawyers read as much as, if not more than, any other professional men. Physicians are poor readers; they keep up with the current medical journals and that is about all. Preachers are little better, if their use of the public library is any criterion; and teachers come to us much less than you would naturally suppose—feeling probably that when their day's work with books is done they want something other than books for relaxation. Night watchmen are frequently our patrons; policemen read pretty regularly; and firemen, who have a lot of time on their hands, often show a familiarity with good books which would put the average business man to blush. Fiction maintains its lead with every group; but the amazing fact is that even the very dullest books in the library are called for by somebody, sometime during the year.

In the same interview he raised the question of the influence of weather upon reading: "Probably if records were kept over a sufficient number of years they would furnish some interesting facts about the different sorts of books that are called for at different periods of the year. At present we have not sufficient data on which to base a general statement. I do think it is true, however, that more folks come to the desk and ask for medical books on dark, gloomy days."

He had a strong feeling that the schools do not stimulate enough of the intellectual toughness that demands what he called "the literature of power."

The study of "literature" does not add much to one's equipment for actual life. Whereas, if education and reading can do anything at all for us they should equip us for to-day.

One may say that this leaves out of sight emotions and enthusiasms and joys which can come from the reading of parts, at least, of the literature of fashion. Not so. Out of the literature of power one can get these same satisfactions; or, if not the same, then joys, emotions and enthusiasms which are better worth having because more fitted to our needs.

By the literature of power is meant, in the first place, the literature of exact knowledge, the literature of science; the literature of fact, not the literature of doctrine; the literature of the only wisdom that is, not the literature of dogma or of superstition.

Included in the literature of power are sound social science; psychology if not over ten years old (written in 1927); philosophy if based on tested facts; exact science and applied science; history; biography, some of it; travel, a little of it. In these and other kindred departments of knowledge are books written by men competent to speak, which appeal to us keenly, broaden us, give us strength for our work; give us knowledge for our daily needs; and give us what the name applied to this class of literature implies—give us power.

Dana in 1926 wrote on "The Pleasant Art of Getting Your Own Library." This pamphlet was republished in 1939. Here, in answer to the question: "Which Are the Books for Me" he sums up his whole approach to one's selection of books to own:

You speak of choosing your friends. You mean that as you meet new people and come to know them you naturally pick out those who appeal to you, who don't bore you, who help you to pass a pleasant evening now and then, who have something new to say, who help you to see things differently and make life more entertaining. You don't pick these friends on sight, and you don't select them on somebody's recommendation. You get to know them first and then hold to them if you like them. Find your own books in the same way.

Dana naturally approached the consideration of education from the point of view of the relation between the school and the library. He was always of the opinion that these twain should be united in a close and continuous co-operation. He wanted to see the library truck at every schoolhouse door and a track from the schools to the library beaten by the feet of both teachers and students. In 1902 he addressed the New Jersey State Teachers Association on "Mere Words."

Words underlie our whole life; are the signs of our nobility and a cause thereof; are bonds of society, the records of our progress and the steps by which we rise. And they are, some of them, as full of emotion as others are of meaning. Association, constant use, experience, story, fable, history, all have made them able to arouse in us sentiments grave and gay, feelings of grief, pity, joy, reverence, emotion, wonder . . . vibrations I may set in motion from my throat, fashioned at my will to make a certain familiar word, can likewise move you, and still more definitely, deeply and permanently than the far more cunningly-fashioned notes of the violin. I will try it. Be as coldly observant and critical as you please—while I simply name to you a few names—it will only make my little experiment the more interesting:

Aladdin, Babylon, the Pyramids, Homer, Ulysses, the Parthenon, the Tiber, Julius Caesar, the Goths, Charlemagne, King Alfred, Richard of the Lion Heart, the Crusades, Napoleon, Waterloo, Lexington, Washington, the Nile, Pharaoh, Moses, Palestine, Herod, the Sea of Galilee, Nazareth, the Garden of Gethsemane, Calvary.

In or with or by those few simple sounds you travelled from Egypt of three thousand years ago down through Greece and Rome and the Middle Ages and modern times to our Revolution, and then went back for a moment to the great figure of all history and to the religion in which you live. Just a handful of words. Consider their power. Mere words!

He went on to show how words in combination have still more power over us, and read parts of the Story of Creation, of the Book of Job and of the Twenty-third Psalm. "Of the power of these phrases to move us I need not speak. We read them, we hear them—and they conquer us." He was driving home his point, that education has not done its full work until it has made us lovers of words, readers. Then he went on to expound his thesis, that the library stands as the companion of the school during the formative years and as a reservoir of learning when school days are over. "The schools are in part established that they may tell the young how to enjoy this feast. They do it. . . . They teach the young to read. They put them in touch with words and phrases; they point out to them the delectable mountains of human thought and action as set forth in 'mere words,' and then they let them go. . . . If now you can bring these young citizens of yours into sympathy with the books the libraries would persuade them to read; if you make 'mere words' inviting to them; if you can impress on them the reading habit; then the libraries can supplement your good work; will rejoice in empty shelves; will feel that they are not in vain; and the coming generation will delight, one and all, in that which good books can give."

It was characteristic of his emphasis upon indigenous interests that he should advocate beginning all teaching of citizenship with instruction in the way in which local institutions are run. He proceeded to put the idea into effect by having experts in the various city departments of Newark prepare simple and brief articles on their work; these he had mimeographed and distributed in the grades where they were studied. At the same time he encouraged a local newspaper editor, Frank J. Urquhart, to prepare a brief history of Newark to be used as a text-book in the schools. In addition to these provisions, he himself prepared a leaflet, *How Boys and Girls Can Help Our City*, which was adapted to older students and emphasized the responsibility of each citizen to take a share in making the city healthy, wholesome and beautiful. He believed in reducing generalizations about civics in favor of factual information about the practical working of the machinery of municipal government.

One suggestion of his hardly calculated to make friends for him among the young was his insistence that schools could be more efficiently and economically run if they operated all the year around. He proposed four terms with two or three days rest between the quarters. Teachers should work throughout the year with as many weeks of vacation as the custom of similar workers would indicate. To offset this he would have given classes work shorter hours during a given day, thus alleviating the teachers' exposure to prolonged strain. The summer term would emphasize organized play, excursions, manual training and gardening. In 1914-15 the experiment of an all-year school was made in Newark, and Dana believed the trial proved his case: "Newark has made the first thorough test of the all-the-year public school method. The test was most successful, and demonstrated that cities can adopt the all-year plan and thereby hasten the progress of children in their studies, improve rather than injure their health, increase the income of teachers without overworking them, increase by nearly 30% the use made of public school buildings and apparatus, thus promoting efficiency without raising the tax-rate, and make it possible for children to cover in the six years from 6 to 12 the course of study, training and discipline now taking the eight years from 6 to 14." In spite of this good report, the experiment has lapsed.

Dana was himself both a tool-user and a man of books. He could not, therefore, align himself with either group in the recurring controversy between advocates of education as manual accomplishment and education as classical mental discipline. The truth of the matter probably is that, here as nearly everywhere else, what is sauce for the goose is not sauce for the gander, but emphases must vary as talents do. Some people get ideas most aptly through their ears, and some through their eyes, and some through their fingers, while all of us know that some memories come most quickly upon contact with certain odors. On the whole, we have built our educational system on aptitudes in hearing and seeing. The child who can hear and remember, or read and remember, is the one who prospers and gains the rewards in a system where recitations and written examinations are the tests. It was natural, therefore, that Dana should have spoken more often of the need of manual expression than of classical training.

At the dedication of the Central Commercial and Manual Training High School in Newark in 1912, the boy from Woodstock spoke in his address: "A healthy boy of 17 without a jack-knife is a moral impossibility, an unmechanical phenomenon, a living witness to the failure of our public schools, and something not to be accepted on faith. . . . To the Yankee mind the pocket knife is essential to the idea of a boy, and this magnificent school is a protest against that unsocial, unnatural, one-sided, maimed conception of a boy without a jack-knife." He saw manual training, however, as something larger than putting a tool in a boy's hand. Newark was a town of skilled labor. Every manufacturer in the city wished he could find competent citizens of the town to work in his shop. Skilled workers had stopped coming from Europe, and Newark was raising no supply of her own. Dana recognized this and advocated more mechanical training as an answer to a social need. He drew for illustration on the experience of Germany: "Germany has taken the units of her population and fitted them with the utmost care to her national needs. She has also the tremendous advantage which rests in the fact that her skilled workers are such by birth, that they form a caste the bonds of which they themselves quietly accept and bear. There is still another advantage with Germany, I mean that relatively large number of highly trained and thoroughly equipped men whom her higher technical schools and universities have turned out." He foresaw the enlistment of American schools in the production of similarly valuable artisans and thought that no revolutionary change in curriculum would be necessary to assure them: "The fact is that the public schools have long been on the right road. Through all the grades manual arts are taught. It will not be difficult to add vocational or trade training to the present curriculum. This country certainly needs a larger supply of men skilled in trades who are content to remain such to the end of their days. To get them it would seem wise to introduce more handwork into all the schools, and to make the schools in general more intimately related to every-day life, more an integral part of modern industrial society."

In spite of the fact that he saw this need so clearly he warned on many occasions against allowing vocational training to absorb the whole school program. As if in answer to a natural objection to what we have just quoted we find him writing on another occasion: "The present strong tendency to put a great part of our public school education into what we call a 'practical' form, making it industrial and vocational, should be yielded to very guardedly. It is a fad, a fashion, a phrase-worship. To some extent it is far worse than a phrase-born fad, for many have cried out in its favor only because they feel that 'vocational' training will supply willing hands for their factories."

His conclusion was: "Our schools should not become lopsided by carrying too much of the handwork side of life into their curriculum. The world needs all kinds of men, students as well as doers. Let us discover and train both." That sounds easy, and it can be done. We have the techniques for discovering aptitudes and developing them. The difficulty is that their application takes money. Our schools run on uniform curricula for all kinds of students because that is the most economical way to work. Like all mass production, it cuts costs. Dana recognized this and pleaded for a new attitude: "I find in New Jersey a certain condescension toward the public schools, accompanied by a certain aloofness . . . the control of schools is in the hands of men who asked to be elected not because they had ability or had had experience but because they wished distinction and desired to enter politics . . . school buildings are not quite up to the modern factory in outward appearance or to a modern tenement in interior finish . . . proximity of wagons and trolley cars make conversation impossible . . .

playgrounds in cellars and yards reduced to narrow lanes.
. . . I venture such criticism because we are doing better
now." He put his finger on the spot when he pointed out
what a democracy can never afford to forget: "The public
schools may be the most effective instrument for general
social betterment, the most powerful agent for promoting
the fine art of living together that mankind has ever created for its improvement."

Being himself a student and reader of Latin, and in particular an admirer of Horace, some of whose works he and
his brother, Dr. Charles, collaborated in translating and
publishing, he was a defender of the intellectual disciplines
and esthetic joys to be gained from knowledge of what
some call the dead languages. In a paper he wrote for the
Dartmouth Alumni Magazine on George P. Marsh 1820, he
cited him as "evidence that the study of Latin, Greek and
mathematics as pursued at Dartmouth for about a hundred
years does not so handicap a man that he cannot rise as
high as his ability and his power of work permit." He
doubted whether modern college apparatus, including even
moving pictures and intercollegiate games, are equally or
any more provocative of the fulfilment of talent.

The procedure he recommended to colleges was to seek
first of all for students of ability and thereafter to construct
and maintain their programs so as to retain these students
and to protect them against diverting influences. He emphasized this conviction because he had come to the conclusion that as a man is born so he is, and there is little the
schools can do about it. "Men are born brilliant, witty,
hopeful, pessimistic, narrow, long-sighted, subordinate,
leaders, and loving or hating responsibility; and no training can give them characteristics other than those with
which they are born. No educational system can do more
than help to develop talent."

Apparently he had his doubts as to whether his own university was maintaining what he remembered as its hospitality toward the unconventional, its nurture of that individuality which he prized as society's asset and talent's assurance. In a letter to a classmate of his he makes his complaint of conditions revealed to him about 1920:

I am sending through Dartmouth my youngest brother's son. I wish you could drop in and let me tell you of certain Dartmouth customs that I discover through him. I can remember that John Fox wore a hat that was not in the fashion, and that Alabama pranced about with a shawl. In these days the young man whom I am looking after will not wear pants in Hanover that do not have cuffs, and insists that he must always dress in a sweater. He nearly wept this morning when I told him he could not have another pair of yellow shoes. Dirty yellow shoes and still dirtier sweater being proper things. Also in summer he must wear white trousers. It does not matter how dirty they are.

All this reminds me of a remark of a social philosopher from England, who visited us and looked us over, to the effect that the only liberty that Americans are now keen about possessing is liberty to be like other folks. Anyone who comes along with the suggestion that he do something different, and especially if he comes along and does something different, gets it in the neck.

Perhaps in our day we were children of circumstances, and trousers that were not long enough and hats that were out of style and shawls instead of overcoats were worn because we must and not because we would; but I do believe that a little of the sense of personal independence was still in existence in Hanover when you and I helped to set the educational and esthetic pace in that intellectual center.

This was a mild complaint, however, compared to that which came when he scented the fact that special privilege was ensconced in the fraternity system at Hanover. Here was an issue that made every drop of his blood boil, and he sounded the trumpet of battle in a letter to Eugene F. Clark, Secretary of Dartmouth College:

Take my special personal grievance—which is paralleled by about half the parents who send boys to Dartmouth—I pay a boy's college expenses supposing that if he is decent and reasonably studious he will have an equal opportunity with all other students to show his abilities and graces in all of college life which lies outside the classroom. I find the assumed equality of opportunity is not there. Certain secret organizations, by combining their forces, take over to their own members, nearly 90% of the opportunities even to compete in college life. Isn't that rotten?—And I have not told it all.

I think I should tell you frankly that I am moved to try to disturb this unbalanced situation, if it is not to be seriously tackled by the authorities. Tell me, is it to go on indefinitely?

From all I have heard the Dartmouth situation is much like that in Princeton, which Wilson fought against. Am I not right?

He supported endowment drives for his old college. But he never accepted an honorary degree from Dartmouth, though it was twice offered. He was consistent at this practice, for he declined also degrees offered by other institutions. In general he felt that, as a people, we had never taken education seriously enough or supported it adequately. Writing to his friend and fellow-Vermonter, Dorothy Canfield Fisher, he expressed his feeling: "Some day this country will discover that until it spends on education about three times that which it now spends it won't get much."

Dana's political pilgrimage carried him from the traditional Republicanism of his home through a period of near-socialistic thinking followed by one of distrust of governmental power to philosophic anarchism. After his first era of devotion to one party he was always an independent voter. He transferred his interest from the machinery of partisan politics, which he looked upon as symptoms, to the two areas of public thinking and social dynamics, which he considered causes. As early as 1911, he wrote:

"The government itself, its form and its personnel, depend for improvement not on themselves and their own activities; but on improvement in the knowledge, habits and sympathies of all the people. These last, then, are what deserve attention. And so some of us have grown into the opinion that one may decline to be inflamed by any one of all possible political parties, and may decline to worship at one leader's shrine or to damn another leader's covenant of legislation, and may even absent himself from primaries and declare that to him a ballot-box bears no close resemblance to a burning bush, and yet may be a proper and useful citizen."

He was a thorough-going democrat in theory and practice and natural reaction. Steeped as he was in the political literature of America he understood the distrust of all political power which was so powerful a force in the minds of the founders of our Republic. Yet he saw clearly the menace to freedom that lies in the economic power vested in wealth and industrial overlordship. He sought for a formula to balance political and economic power. Nevertheless, he realized that the sheer momentum of events was forcing new patterns of relationships throughout all society, and that important changes would come without waiting upon men or platforms.

In a letter to Professor Thomas Reed Powell of Columbia University he summed up one side of his thinking:

It may interest you to know that it took me about ten years to pass from the Black Republicanism of Vermont with its marvellously efficient method—the protective tariff—of making us a nation of government-worshippers to what one might call societism. This was long ago and the years have intensified my feeling that a nation that looks government-ward is surely slowing up and probably is running down!

For years we have moved steadily toward federal control (which is socialism, of course). To-day we are moving toward it at terrific speed. Is it possible that we shall reach the extreme of the pendulum-swing within so short a space as a few months; that the governing group of men will be so drunk with power that they will push the movement on, and that, hence, we may get a return swing started—through revulsion of feeling, perhaps partly aroused by the sight of governmental failure—far sooner than we now dare hope?

This letter was written in 1918.

Deeply as he felt about the folly of governmental absolutism, however, he saw events in too wide a frame to blame political tendencies on individual men in power. For in the same year he wrote to *The New Republic* giving a broad account of the social causes of political readjustment:

I have long been of the few who believe that the secret of social advance, of increasing the sum total skill in living together with a maximum of comfort and pleasure for all, lies not in the modifications of the forms and manners of government, but in the modifications of the minds, habits and emotions of the nation's component units.

. . . we are entering on an era of growth of superstition in the domain of government . . . the social order, including all the forms of speech and action of everyone of us, is daily changing under the impact of circumstance with which the Constitution has nothing to do, and against which no constitution, however cunningly devised, can avail one whit. The changes thus going on are not born of laws or politics or parties; they are born of us and are fathered by circumstances. They modify our federal constitution daily and daily overturn our laws.

This letter was written in support of Mr. Croly's suggestion that a school of social research be established. It was another affirmation of a conviction Dana once phrased more picturesquely: "I have a remedy. It is education. But it's damned slow in operation, and the Philistines be upon thee, Samson!"

Beneath all bewilderment, however, Dana carried one immutable conviction:

Though we seem to win, we lose all if we lose our Liberty. Our Liberty lies in the faith that our Nation is a State of Mind. The State of Mind is a quiet certitude that every man should be permitted to pursue his own aims, letting all others pursue theirs; that no rule of man by man is good or can long endure; that the only worthy conquest is conquest of one's self. If in our fight we lose this faith we are neither free nor friends of freedom, and Democracy is lost, not saved.

Creeds are at best formal statements of belief arising out of the particular events that prompted their formulation, and so carry emphases that are dated. Nevertheless they are revelatory of the minds that produce them, for while immediate debate may define the issue the prevailing characteristics of the writer will be revealed in the implications he reads into it. Dana was no man for creedal anchors, but once he did attempt to catch his rules of conduct into words:

I wish to be kind, just, intelligent, diligent and happy, and to persuade others to help me so to be; because I know that in so far as I succeed I shall help my country to be generous, law-abiding, prosperous and progressive; a country in which everyone may find so much pleasure as his own nature permits him to earn and to enjoy.

If my country does wrong, I shall oppose it in that wrong. If any try to injure it, I shall oppose them and, if need be, I shall fight them.

I believe that we are and should continue united in the task of making everyone each day more nearly equal before our laws, our customs, and our opinions, and in giving to everyone every day greater freedom in thought and speech and action; all to the end that all may work together in harmony and in mutual aid to make this a still more desirable dwelling place for a gentle, intelligent and industrious people.

He was not an absolute pacifist, but his mind revolted against war and repudiated its glorification. He anticipated that the reason would eventually find a better way of settling disputes. To his friend, Richard C. Jenkinson, president of his Board of Trustees, who had advised against accepting any guns or other warlike objects to decorate the Library grounds, he expressed his agreement: "as to war monuments, cannon and such, I am immensely pleased to know that you are as much against them as I am. Their day is going by and I am almost led to believe that the move against war will astonish us with its strength, even before you and I are gone." Even during the War, he refused to make such concessions to popular passion as he could not justify to his own rational integrity. German books stayed on the Library's shelves as evidence that a contemporary struggle could blot out neither past accomplishment nor future promise in the fields of universal culture.

The years that saw the beginnings of the World War were also the ones in which new problems of labor were making themselves felt in the United States. In 1914 Christian W. Feigenspan, brewer and large employer, wrote to Dana asking for light on labor practices:

The general trend of paternalism in governments, as I see it, leads me to believe that we are retarding the progress which working men have made under the day system, and is giving them a lead back to the time when once more we shall legislate not only what we shall do for them in the way of providing for their care during illness resulting from injuries sustained during the course of their employment, old age pensions which will provide for them after they have become useless as a working unit, and widows' pensions in the event of not having made sufficient provisions for their families at their death, but a great many other things, which will mean that the workman is on the road to where he was, and that we shall again, if we continue along this path, see the day when we shall have the two classes—and one will be the slave.

Dana's answer was to point out that the laws in question were written to correct evils presently irritating and demanding rectification:

The Dartmouth College case in 1819 decided that the charters of corporations are unalterable by the authority that granted them save with the consent of the corporations themselves. The employed, being unable to curtail directly the prodigious power of these artificial, deathless, highly privileged and monopolizing persons—chartered corporations—have attempted to check them by countless laws which seem to be, and often are, productive of far more harm to the business of the corporation than of good to the employed and the general public. . . . When I look at this legislation as being curative of present improper conditions, as limiting the arbitrary power of those persons who have great wealth, endless life, and special powers which the State cannot curtail, they seem rather beneficial.

The danger, he felt, was that of too great a dependence on the government to promote the general welfare. "Every new bit of legislation that seems for a time to make the common man's lot more tolerable strengthens the ancient habit of submission. And as the habit of submission grows, the practice of oppression grows also—and the new slavery." He did not like the tyranny of laws. Once he poured out his distrust of overlegalization in an article entitled: "The Bad Habit of Having Law Makers and Lawyers." He described the law as a habit that had become partly a superstition; and suggested that we must outgrow it as we have outgrown cannibalism, slavery and polygamy. Lawmakers, he thought, could not be otherwise than blunderingly, even maliciously, harmful when he considered their manner of selection. He called the lawyer class the most powerful and self-assertive of labor unions. In conclusion, he called upon lawyers themselves to lessen the harm their existence causes by attacking in an organized way the hurtful habit of worshipping the law.

Naturally he found himself opposed on principle to any invasion by the law into areas of private decision. Thus he was vigorously opposed to Prohibition and the Volstead Act. To the *Vermont Standard,* he wrote:

The "Woodstock Column" referred recently to the *Minute Men,* strongly hinting that it is a vile if not a wicked sheet. I am proud to say that I am one of the sponsors of that journal and a member of the organization for the abolition of the 18th amendment. . . . I write this in behalf of common sense and that principle of individual action which goes well with individual responsibility which Vermonters were long supposed to uphold, and I am glad to sign it.

Nor did he look upon individual rights as prerogatives of the male of the species. Among his papers is a note which reads: "Every woman should be trained for a job. Every woman who knows enough to do it should take advantage of every possible opportunity to promote the independence of women. No young woman should be expected to stay at home and take care of her parents with any greater degree of expectancy than is extended to the young men of the family."

Human beings are ends in themselves. Society is people co-operating for their mutual advantage. Government is a means to serve individual and social ends; and when it becomes more is tyranny. These were his premises. In all his journeyings his mind never experimented with foundations less stable than the stern simplicity of his native hills.

CHAPTER XI

CITY AND REGIONAL PLANNING

IN the nearly thirty years that Dana spent in Newark the city passed through a period of change in population, in industrial organization, in the distribution of national groups, and in transportation that left the city of 1929 a much different social unit from that which he had found in 1902. At the turn of the century it was still a big country town with old and established families dominating its social and political life and the traditional Protestant churches founded in colonial days maintaining their central places in its culture; thirty years later it was an industrial city from which the majority of the leaders in its commerce had moved into the suburbs, transferring their social and political influences with them, while large numbers of Catholics and Jews had moved into Newark to exert influences sufficiently strong to displace the older religious establishments from their traditional leadership. The population increased in numbers from some 250,000 to 400,000. The newcomers were largely people of foreign birth who came with the waves of immigration that marked the two decades from 1900–1920. Meanwhile, the convenient location of Newark and the development of electrical power had attracted industries and initiated new enterprises; such powerful establishments as The Public Service Company, the New Jersey Bell Telephone Company, Bamberger's Department Store, the insurance companies, The Weston Electrical Instrument Company, and many others began or had phenomenal growth during this time. In nearly all cases, however, the heads of these companies lived and voted outside the city, so that the actual residents and voters were more and more of the wage-earning groups. Their national origins were widely contrasted: German (attracted by brewing interests and other demands for skilled laborers), Irish, Italian, Russian, Polish, and Lithuanian; the World War period saw the beginning of the Negro influx which had brought the number of these citizens up to 10% of the city's population (1939). At the same time, tubes and bridges and better highways were steadily forging more intimate contacts with New York and, simultaneously, weaving the whole region into one web of residential and communal unity.

Because the boundaries of the city had long been fixed, no geographical expansion was possible. This meant that increased population forced maximum use of existing property which resulted in concentration of social problems. These, in turn, called for heavy municipal expenditures added to the normal ones incident to necessary improvements and additions to public buildings. City government became expensive, taxes rose, politics became increasingly dominant while the proportion of large tax-payers to resident-voters declined. Behind all this, however, was the basic problem of building an American community out of heterogeneous families of many contrasting conditions.

In 1930, the year after Dana died, the population of Newark was 442,337. Of these 287,392, or 65%, were native whites, but 50% of these were of wholly foreign parentage. The foreign born whites numbered 115,204 or 26% of the whole population, while negroes were 9%. Moreover, the illiterates, 10 years old and over, were 5% of the total number.

Such a city, undergoing a bewildering metamorphosis, was the one on which Dana as one of its citizens looked.

He saw it. The Library and Museum were his two main channels of activity to help it. But he did not stop with them. He assumed the responsibilities of an active participant in wider civic activities. To begin with, he set himself the task of making the city acquainted with and proud of itself. He stimulated writing about Newark. Mr. Urquhart not only wrote the history of Newark already mentioned but others telling of its founding and its famous men. Mayor Thomas Raymond wrote an appreciation of Stephen Crane, and Max Herzberg followed this with books and articles on Crane and other literary figures associated with Newark. The Carteret Book Club, composed of book-lovers and collectors of the city, was organized and it published volumes dealing with local history, including an elaborate monograph on the city illustrated by Rudolph Ruzicka and written by Walter Pritchard Eaton. Christian W. Feigenspan gave a superb copy of Verocchio's Colleoni to be set up in Lincoln Park. All these were inspired or encouraged by Dana.

He, himself, edited and published through the Library, *The Newarker*, a periodical which not only interpreted his own institutions but carried information about all sides of the city's life. It became in his hands a current guide to all that was going on, a first aid to the perception of local objects of beauty and interest, an introduction to city planning, and a continual spur to civic pride. Month by month it carried to its readers some of the insatiable curiosity and versatile opinions of its editor.

Comparing the three cities in which he had worked, he once remarked: "Denver was discovered, Springfield was inherited, but Newark is a city thrust upon its people." However cities come, they get their dimensions at a price. The town in the Rocky Mountains demanded its toll of pioneer extravagance; the city of Massachusetts grew by the long and steady pull of generations; and Newark had to foot its bills, only quickly like a boy buying a completely new outfit of clothes because his former ones are suddenly too small. Dana wrote in *The Newarker* of how great the price must be:

The burden of Newark's expenses grows daily and will continue to grow. Many things make it inevitable . . . growth of population . . . growth in effectiveness as a city . . . rise of the standard of living. . . . The growth of expenditures of this city in the next thirty years is inevitable.

Foreseeing this, he was active in promoting a City Plan Commission. Largely due to his efforts Mayor Haussling appointed a commission of nine citizens on June 1, 1911. Dana was a member and for four years he was its most active spirit. Experts were engaged and reports formulated on the City Market, traffic, street paving, housing, commercial signs, transportation, recreation facilities and new streets. Surveys were also presented of harbor development, manufacturing and industrial plants, and educational needs. In so far as Newark has safeguarded community values in its intense physical developments, the work of this commission has been its guide. Such planning was unusually compatible with his mental slant. When an exhibit was to be set up at the Museum or the Library he would visualize it in exact detail before work on it was begun. When he proposed any projects for meeting social needs he would carefully prepare a blue-print of the desired organization. Every one of his activities he approached as an engineer approaches a piece of construction. His city was changing and he was one who wanted no haphazard development but a planned pattern of growth to assure conservation of all community values.

Obviously, reports and surveys would not guarantee results. So he used every means of publicity to guide the public to understanding and approval. He spoke frequently, turning every occasion into a suitable argument

for creative community thinking. He wrote frequent letters
to the newspapers making passing events his texts for driving home principles of permanent benefit. He set up City
Plan exhibitions to answer the question: How shall we
make Newark a more efficient city? Through a steady
stream of pamphlets flowing into the public schools he
kept alive youthful interest. And *The Newarker* steadily carried his gospel of civic betterment. He aroused enough
interest to improve many conditions. Fortunately, Mayor
Thomas Raymond was a lover of books and so became a
staunch friend of Dana who, in turn, was able to guide the
mayor's indisputable political ability into many useful enterprises. Both the Library and the city profited from their
close association. By 1919, Dana was able to write: "In
these last fifteen years my own city has made itself anew.
It is now quite clean, hygienic and wholesome. It is quite
well managed. It rapidly grows more attractive. It is, in
view of its situation, wonderfully self-conscious. And nearly
all this is in sharp contrast to the conditions of 1904." And
in 1926, he could say with even more enthusiasm: "Whatever Newark was a few decades ago, she is now a real city,
with a soul and with every promise of becoming all that
her most optimistic friends dream of her becoming."

He felt deeply about Newark. Occasionally his normal
quiet speech would burst into a genuine poetry as his emotions gained the upper hand. Love has its own answer to
those who think it blind:

The view at sunset south and down the river from the Bridge
Street bridge is a thing of glory.

The western bank is in heavy shadow as the sun gets low. That
huge trestle of steel, crowned with a derrick, and designed merely
to pass lime, sand and other gross elements of skyscrapers swiftly
to and fro, looks like a monstrous centipede parading the river's
bank and guarding the three vast circular towers beyond. The

towers are gas tanks at midday—now they are the huge keeps of a gigantic castle, which casts its shadows over the dark waters below. Beyond are slender monuments, not mere chimneys in this light; but shafts set to immortalize the river's good spirits.

Slender columns rise in the distance, like those of a Greek temple, but more slender and more beautiful, and in actual fact steel chimneys set to the easy task of drawing east wind through furnaces below.

The sun's rays accentuate the stable squareness of the memorial shafts, the beautiful roundness of the distant Greek columns, and of the high towers of the castles; they sharpen the outlines of the huge shops ranked right and left down the stream and cast softening shadows over all the ruck of gable, derrick, pier and scaffold along the western bank.

It is a view all Newarkers may delight in. They may first find joy in it simply as a vision of delight, and then, if they must, they may take pleasure in the thought of the busy and profitable life of the men who have builded it all.

Dreaming over his city, probing its problems, stimulating its thinking, and planning its development, Dana watched restlessly over its streets, selflessly winning recognition as Newark's first citizen.

Men used often to say that Massachusetts is a state of mind. With equal justice, New Jersey may be described as a state of suspension. It is drawn to and dependent upon New York at one end and Philadelphia at the other. This natural division of interest has been emphasized by historical attitudes inherited from colonial days when the proprietary compromises split the colony north and south. To this day the men of South Jersey have a kind of fierce pride in their locality akin to that of Virginians in the Old Dominion, and it expresses itself in a distrust of the interlopers, considered nought but merchants and New York men, of the northern part of the State. Their fine scorn has been lessened no whit by the growth of political power and political machines in the hands of men essentially strange to them.

This lends a certain picturesqueness to the life of a State which is full of contrasts—the Sussex hills against the marshy flats, plutocratic Llewellyn Park against the abject section of the Pines—but it does not help create a unity of outlook for New Jersey as a whole. Moreover, the commuters from New York and Philadelphia have at best a limited interest in the State that is their bedroom. They do not think of themselves as Jerseymen, in fact a large number of them never read a newspaper published in the State of their residence, and, therefore, rely for their information about it on the incidental items contained in journals whose primary interest is elsewhere, and whose occasional editorials on its affairs are usually couched in the faintly mocking tones that superiors reserve for those whom they patronize and wish indulgently to encourage.

Thus do history and environmental factors conspire to defeat the growth of civic solidarity among the people of this State that was one of the original thirteen colonies, and the only one among them to have two colleges within its borders. To Dana, with his intense belief in the value of loyalties indigenous to the soil, a State that grew none of the virtues that come from love of a local habitation and a home presented a baffling environment. He became an exponent and exhorter of the state spirit. At the dedication of the Trenton Library, he was already defining the issue:

New Jersey lacks proper pride. Her own people tell me this and I fear it is so. If true, it is easily explained; though not easily justified. Since its very foundation, our state has looked east to New York and west to Philadelphia, two great centers of human interest. New Jersey has a rich and full historic background. But always the interests of the restless, active and progressive intellects among her people have been drawn toward the great cities just beyond her borders.

He did not rest with this statement. Shortly after it he sent out a circular throughout the State requesting help in locating material conducive to encouraging civic sentiment of State-wide dimensions:

In connection with our work with the schools, we have been looking for literary material having to do with New Jersey,—sketches of prominent men, stories of dramatic incidents, descriptions of interesting historical spots, etc., in prose and poetry. Thus far we have found very little indeed. Has none of New Jersey's history got into the field of belles lettres? Do you know of any?

Little response came to this request. Accordingly, in an informal speech to a group of librarians, he declared that "of literature of the first class, referring to New Jersey men and scenes and incidents, there is none." This remark was widely quoted, and aroused a good deal of comment and resentment. Since then, Eugene R. Musgrove has collected a volume of *Poems of New Jersey* (1923), various biographies of prominent Jerseymen have appeared, and the New Jersey Historical Society and other local groups organized around historical events (notably the Washington Association at Morristown) have gathered and published state data of importance. The raw materials for producing pride in New Jersey now exist, and to Dana must go much of the credit for its appearing.

In a speech at Westfield he made a strong plea for making the young conscious of their state's history and resources:

We cannot gain seclusion . . . but we can do more than we have to develop the habit of "Looking at New Jersey." Most of the elders . . . will continue to wear in their eyes the far-away look acquired by daily gazing at Manhattan from the forward deck of a

ferry-boat; most of them will continue to have. . . . the "Garbage
Can Myopia" which makes all streets look beautiful so long as they
are open for navigation. But here are the young . . . we must place
in the hands of the teachers and the children the means of becoming acquainted with our State. The story of New Jersey should
come to them in poetry, in song, in simple record, in picture and
through museums, in samples of her rocks, soils, birds, plants, ani-
mals, minerals, and her thousand products of factory and field.

When he himself "looked at New Jersey" he saw at least
one improvement that could be made. It could have "a
cleaner face." He suggested as part of the cleansing process
"the elimination of the signs which perch like vultures on
our landscape." "You remember the foolish and perverse
generation in the Bible which vainly asked for signs. An observant friend of mine says: 'It's no wonder they couldn't
get any signs, New Jersey had 'em all!' "

The generally indifferent attitude of the state's population, combined with the fact of its relatively great wealth,
has made it an easy setting for political machines able to
support a steadily voting number of dependents. The industrial leaders have found it more economical to accept
these machines than to fight them. Consequently, New
Jersey politics, as Woodrow Wilson so bitterly learned,
holds small regard for men who know other motives than
selfish gain. The usual parties appear on the ballots, but
apparent rivalry does not hinder profitable cooperation.
Any political boss of the moment is too realistic to permit
partisan disputes to check his participation in the successes
of another party when its candidate is a reasonable man.
He prefers the convenient arrangement which leaves the
voters free to choose their own man as long as whichever
one they choose is his. In such a setting, independent men
are baffled by the futility of party matters until the popular
mind revolts against boss-rule and rises up to overthrow it.

Dana hated the system that ruled his state, but recognized the peculiar limitations of his position that made it impossible for him to align himself with any political crusades.

Meanwhile, however, there were state agencies doing scientific work that had no partisan bias, but did offer guidance to wise state policies. He supported these and counted it among his duties to promulgate their findings. The Library publicized their activities and often housed exhibitions displaying their data. He particularly praised the State Department of Conservation and Development:

> The work of a department of this kind seems to suffer from lack of intensive interest on the part of intelligent citizens. Almost any business man in New Jersey will give his time and thought freely to the discussion of partisan politics and the election to high office of his own particular candidate. Would he but divert a part of that attention to the work of the State Department of Conservation and Development as outlined in reports and other publications, we would have a little less of politics, which some might lament, but we should have a better state in all respects.

He was a lonely prophet in the preaching of New Jersey's self-respect. The restless flux of moving shifts of population, the magnetic preoccupation with a neighboring metropolis, the spasmodic and incidental interest in local affairs, and the unsleeping vigilance of those who have made a personal business of the state's public life have combined to work more powerfully than his words. His insight would have saved the State from its confusion, and prevented the blackest of its shame, but wisdom lacking attention is mere wind, and New Jersey is not yet ready to learn how to be a community.

Granting everything that has been said, however, about local interest and pride it still remains true that down-town Newark is nearer to New York's City Hall than outlying sections of the great metropolis itself, and that several

counties of New Jersey look across the Hudson at the tow-
ered and broken profile of Manhattan. Economically and
socially the urban area of northern Jersey and the metropolitan area of New York are a unit; politically they are
divided by the state line which has been the more formi-
dable because it has had the wide fjord of the Hudson River
as its marker. A typical social lag has made political and
geographical division more potent than economic unity
in determining psychological attitudes, so that planning
on a regional basis did not enter the minds of responsible
men in earlier days.

Since 1900, however, the improvement of highways and
the achievement of the Hudson Tunnels have made travel
throughout the region swifter. Not only has New York been
brought closer to New Jersey, but the northern counties of
the state itself have been more intimately interwoven. This
has resulted in new building, in the development of subur-
ban communities, and in the urbanization of a continually
widening area. To-day (1939) the department stores of
Newark serve a population of two million people. Dana
early saw a development like this was bound to come.
Characteristically, he believed that its progress should be
planned. In 1906 he was chairman of the Interurban Committee of the Newark Board of Trade, and issued a thirty-
page printed report with maps devoted to "Northern New
Jersey considered as part of the Port of New York." The
opening sentences are:

Contiguous to New York Harbor and including the southern counties of the State of New York and the northern counties of New
Jersey there is rapidly being evolved a metropolitan community
which, within a single generation, will have become the greatest
city of the world. Its rate of growth and development is accelerated
each year by improvements in transportation, and also by the
dawning realization of the wonderful possiblities of its future.

The responsibilities of citizenship at this, the most critical and formative period in the history of the community, are as great as they are interesting, since we are now just beginning to understand what is impending and since the obstructions which the Hudson and East rivers and the Hackensack Meadows have heretofore imposed upon local development are about to be removed. The entire metropolitan district henceforth will develop as a whole and not separately as Long Island and New Jersey with a city between them. To provide for this development so that it shall be balanced, correlated and symmetrical—so that the most shall be made of natural opportunities and natural disadvantages minimized—so that the resulting metropolis shall in effect become efficient and beautiful, as well as the most powerful municipality in the world, constitutes the end to be attained.

He proposed a comprehensive development plan to supersede local plans of separate communities dominated by parochial and personal interests. In great detail he discussed the use of the meadows, the possibilities of the Kills and Newark Bay, plans for transportation and trunk lines, bridges, water supply, streets and parks, buildings, advertising signs, and methods of control. A large bird's-eye view of the Port of New York supplied the key to his recommendations.

Following this report the Interurban Association of Northeastern New Jersey, with delegates from several Boards of Trade, was organized in the Spring of 1907. Dana was elected chairman. Ten years later, the Chamber of Commerce of the State of New York devoted a meeting to the discussion of greater cooperation between New York and New Jersey, particularly in the development of the metropolitan area regardless of state or county lines. Governor Walter E. Edge of New Jersey and Comptroller William A. Prendergast of New York City spoke. As a result of this meeting, and upon action by the legislatures of the two states, the New York, New Jersey Port and Harbor

Development Commission was organized. It made an exhaustive study and recommended the creation of a Central Bi-State Port Authority. Governor Alfred E. Smith of New York enthusiastically supported it. Eventually The Port of New York Authority was legally created, and it is the body which has, among other activities, built the Holland and Lincoln Tunnels and the George Washington Bridge. Although Dana served on neither the Development Commission nor the Port Authority, he thus saw a part of his regional plan brought into active operation through other hands.

CHAPTER XII

HABITS, INTERESTS, AND HOBBIES

MANY of our American leaders have been ingenious tool-users as well as men of ideas—so many that we might almost cite this as typical of our national life. Benjamin Franklin was an expert mechanic and his experiment with the lightning is enough to attest his ingenuity. Thomas Jefferson loved to tinker with gadgets and the continuance of some of his contrivances in practical use to-day is evidence of his genuine inventive skill. We do not need to multiply examples, they will readily occur to our minds. The explanation may lie in the fact that ours is a country that hitherto has drawn its leadership from the farms. When a harness breaks or a blade gets dull, the farmer has to fix them himself, or did have to before the days of telephones and automobiles. He was forced to be handy and ingenious. Also, we have been a country without an aristocracy so that our leaders have perforce come from the ranks of workers. Even our earliest Presidents, for example, were such as came from close working with tools and the soil. George Washington, wealthy and aristocratic as we think him, had been a poor boy carrying his surveyor's chain over the Fairfax lands and remained to the end of his life primarily a farmer at heart as his singularly disarming diary shows.

Or, perhaps there is such a distinct group among men as the manually minded, and these have been preeminent among us. Hamilton, on the other hand, was no tool-user at all, but the product of another kind of environment. In later times, Theodore Roosevelt might be counted among the manually adept, but Woodrow Wilson not. Taken collectively, however, our leaders would probably show a larger proportion of men who found pleasure in their own manual skills than would those of any Western nation in the past century and a half. We have drawn upon the ranks of the farmers, the cobblers, the rail-splitters. Lately, we have specialized in lawyers and professors, but they are still an experiment and not yet a tradition.

I

Dana was in the tradition of the tool-users. Not only did he like to print, setting his own sticks of type, but he used all kinds of tools. He made tables and chairs. He designed and built model boxes for carrying objects from his institutions to the schools, arranging them so that they could be displayed without removing them from the boxes. He experimented with the construction of bookcases and designed one suitable for the average man's library of perhaps fifty books. Both in Newark and at Woodstock he had a complete carpenter's shop.

On his farm at Woodstock he built and repaired the pieces of equipment as any farmer would. In one of his letters he reports: "I've just remade a wheelbarrow. My creative work is seen chiefly in a Windmill, which is visited only a little less than is Calvin Coolidge's house thirteen miles away. And my Windmill, tho' a mere machine, is a d—d sight more worthy of a visit than is C. C.'s home— even when C. C. is there!"

His farm was organized as expertly as the Newark Library. "The pigs were neatly labelled on their leather backs, and the chickens accounted for in a card catalogue," as the Newark *News* slyly reported. During his vacation weeks he followed a regular farm routine, hoeing his garden, tending his growing crops and milking his four Holstein cows. Some people advised him to give up general farming and go in exclusively for maple sugar, but he preferred to cultivate the land. Incidentally, he must have enjoyed a chuckle when a reporter duly recorded for posterity that he did not choose to raise maple sugar because he believed "that continual cultivation of cane would weaken his land"; and the bucolic preference: "Mr. Dana's favorite book is 'Mrs. Wiggs of the Cabbage Patch.'"

For two years he was a member of the Executive Committee of the Windsor County Fair and got so enthusiastically into the spirit of it that he boasted of it as "the best County Fair in New England." He also wrote to the local papers on occasional agricultural subjects. In a more practical mood he sent letters to publishers of agricultural journals asking them to send "to the farmers named on the list enclosed, one or more copies of your journal, or such publications of your organization, as you may think would be helpful to these people." His correspondence is dotted with notes from his office in the city discussing affairs at the farm: "I have written Dick Marble about doing some things, and am writing him to-day to put in some Little Marvel peas as soon as he can. Tell him I either use a double row or I make one row 8″ to 10″ wide and put in an awful lot of peas, and if he will do it I shall be pleased." Again, ordering some trees he commented: "I have a shagbark hickory which bears very poor nuts not worth growing; but even the shagbark hickory of this type is not common in my part of Vermont." In a different vein he wrote to the Editor of the *Vermont Standard* in Woodstock:

I hear from my brother, Harold S. Dana of Woodstock, that he is making a scratch-run for his famous aggregation of hens, and that he is covering this run with the new glass-cloth which I find widely advertised.

I write to ask readers of *The Standard* to tell my brother at once if any of them know of any injurious effects produced by this glass-cloth. It is guaranteed to permit the violet rays—which are strongly actinic and produce a very great effect on the average hen—to go through and light upon the hen or hens as the case may be. Naturally I am alarmed over the possible outcome;—for what effect would this treatment of the hens have upon their product if they laid blue eggs?

It is needless to say that I consulted our State Ornithologist, Mr. Pember, and have verified what he says by consultation with Mr. R. Woods; and he, Mr. Pember, replies that he does not know among all the birds of his acquaintance a single hen; in fact has never heard of it. This is probably the highest-browed State Ornithologist there is in the world.

But my inquiry about blue eggs is serious.

At home at his bench the Vermont boy with a jack-knife took control, and ever and again the sweet winds from the hills of the North blew into the office of the librarian. Clean wood and the brown earth made his fingers work with a skill that communicated its own delight to his spirit.

II

Dana had pleasure in good conversation: "I decided years ago that while the most entrancing of all indulgences is reading, and while the most futile and in some respects most injurious of all forms of human intercourse is the lecture, the most improving and on the whole most enjoyable of all occupations is rational conversation between intelligent people." Unfortunately, conversations are like the sand which the tide washes away. Except for a few men— Johnson, Coleridge, Carlyle, Goethe, Socrates perhaps— we have but sparse records of those extemporary self-revelations that men make in the excitement of good talk. We are likely to get the distilled essence of a mind, its wine, in prepared books and papers, but the native flavor, the grape, escapes us.

In a group of Dana's friends the question of his conversations came up, and in the attempt to characterize them members of the company said that they were "intellec-

tual," "versatile," "wise"; somebody seeking a more precise statement ventured: "sympathetic, no, kindly, yet
something more, perhaps understanding is the word." This
was not fully accepted for it seemed too soft and the remark
was made: "You do not describe him unless you emphasize that he was just, stubbornly fair, so to speak." Another
suggested: "He talked positively, fully conscious of his own
powers"; and still another: "I think that if I had to restrict
myself to one word it would be, refreshing."

His natural speech was quiet and, while not slow, was
not impulsive. He could discuss Horace, as he loved to do,
or tell how to grow asparagus or make a whistle. He took
his own wide range of interests so naturally for granted
that he was surprised when others could not easily follow
him through all of them; one young woman still remem-
bers his startled question: "What? You don't know about
Diesel engines?" His expectation that she would was a part
of the genuine simplicity, in the sense of absence of pretentiousness, that marked him. He took his own curiosity
as given in the premises and presumed that other minds
had an equal capacity for exploration.

He was a good listener. "People tell me all their troubles," he used to say; and he was wise enough to know that
most people solve their own difficulties when they have
talked them out. Young people found a champion in him,
and he was seldom too busy to give time to such as came
genuinely inquiring. "He always spoke to me if he saw me
in the Library," is one man's recollection, "and usually
asked me what I was reading, and why." With learners he
was imperturbably patient, but he dropped the lazy like
hot cakes.

A visitor to the Library some ten years after his death,
hearing his name so often and realizing how his influence
persisted, asked the question: "Doesn't the ghost walk too

much?" Unconsciously she was paying her posthumous tribute to the remarkable loyalty he won from his closest associates. Those who worked most intimately with him came to have a deep respect that can be described in no less moving phrase than actual affection for him. Their various temperaments—the executive energy of Beatrice Winser, the luminous enthusiasm of Holger Cahill, the logical excellence of Marguerite Gates, the technical thoroughness of Alice Kendall, the reliable skill of Katherine Coffey—all found affirmation and support in him. On one occasion, John Evans, who acted as his chauffeur, talked to me about him, and in his Irish speech were present the same accents of profound regard as colored all expressions of those who saw him most closely. From the engineers to the expert professionals, all associated with him found in his spirit a flame that kindled their own.

When he spoke in public, which he did sparingly, his manner was conversational. He distrusted oratory and refused what seemed to him its specious artifices. Nevertheless, he commanded attention. His tall, slightly stooped frame crowned with a well-shaped head, out of which two brilliant eyes looked, gave him an impressive appearance. The authority of his own position and accomplishments, along with his reputation for original ideas, put his audiences in the mood to listen. So he usually spoke with genuine effect, being at his best in the midst of debate.

III

His humor, like his speech, was quiet. It was of the New England Yankee kind, as when he put on his exhibition of pottery from the five-and-ten-cent-stores keeping its origin a secret till the objects had been admired, or when he said he could not raise maple sugar because the cane would impoverish the ground. Sometimes, emerging from his office in company with his associates, he would let out a yell that would reverberate through all the careful library halls, and then he would chuckle mischievously at the shocked expressions on the faces beside him.

On one occasion he found himself idly fingering his fonts of type matching examples of each against the rest in an orderly stick until a sentence formed itself under his hand:

THIS OUR NOBLE ART

And this our noble art of Printing is the very Foster Mother of all Learning; for though the few had Books before Gutenberg gave us our Art, not until Printing came could Learning, yes and Wisdom also, knock at every man's door.

To this he added:

From the Latin of Cardelius, 1546.

He made several copies for distribution among his friends, some of whom hung them on their office walls. On April 1, 1909 a letter appeared in *The Nation* asking: "Who was Cardelius?" Two weeks later one Robert Restiaux replied: "He was a native of Franconia. . . . One of his works best known in his day is on the virtues of garlic, another on the spread of polite literature among the peasant classes, and a third on the diseases that affect bookworms." On May 8 a correspondent signing himself Harmon Karl professed pain that so erroneous an account of "the master" had found its way into print. "Frankenau" was his native place; and not garlic, but "sorrel—common or garden sorrel— a herb now much neglected for its savor, but formerly highly esteemed and much used," was the subject of his best known work. "A Respectful Enquirer" wrote that so obviously pedantic an author as Cardelius seemed to be could not have written the lucid sentence on the noble art of printing, and suggested that the name was a misprint for that of "John Cardelinus, the famous jurist of Bologna, husband of the beautiful and learned Novella." On May 1, 1909 one Beverly Buncombe of North Carolina asserted that Cardelius was no Frenchman or German but an American, and that it was time the previous correspondents "and your other readers learn a few elementary principles of true Americanism." "He is a native born citizen of Buncombe County in this state and I have had the honor of an interview with him this very morning. . . . Colonel Cardelius would have said nothing about the matter, but I was determined that justice should be done to one of our most eminent citizens." The obvious herb that claimed the Colonel's erudition was the mint, an ingredient of a popular local beverage. On May 21, Dana told the true story, and complimented *The Inland Printer* on its use of the quotation, elaborately decorated, as the frontispiece of its May issue. Subsequently it appeared that Robert Restiaux was Henry W. Kent, Harmon Karl was Edward H. Virgin, the Respectful Enquirer was Ruth Grannis, and Beverly Buncombe was Edmund L. Pearson. William E. A. Axon of Southport, England wrote *The Nation* in July that he had been "much puzzled by the quotation from the pseudo-Cardelius, for I was at that time occupied with a genuine fifteenth century poem in honor of the first printer." A somewhat mordant touch is given this whole amusing prank of Dana and his friends by one of his laments about the stodginess of Newark's thinking: "Where shall I find one man in this place who reads *The Nation*, to whom I can talk of what appears in its pages?"

The Newark Academy Alumni Association asked him to speak at its twenty-first annual dinner. For this occasion he prepared a mock-heroic poem that drew its inspiration from the early days of 1810 when the Academy had girls as well as boys enrolled, and particularly from the admirable record of one, Elizabeth Pintard Boudinot. Half amus-

ing, half shaming his hearers, Dana read them such lines
as these:

> *The Academic fashion Plato set*
> *Is, here by Newark's marshes, followed yet.*
>
> .   .   .   .   .   .
>
> *The perfect City, too, these sages sought,*
> *(Of Boards of Trade, alas! they had not thought!)*
> *Of his ideal Republic, Plato spoke,*
> *Where Public Service was no Public Joke!*
> *Where zeal for public welfare all inspired*
> *And business men of Business sometimes tired.*
>
> *You recognize the place? The Greek's ideal*
> *No more's a dream, for Newark's made it real!*
>
> .   .   .   .   .   .

Humorously, he related the accomplishments of "our Par-
agon," Eliza Boudinot, and then turned to point the moral
that the Academy men had received much of their city and
owed it much in returns, at least enough:

> *In public progress as in private needs*
> *(To) put "A Better Newark" in your creeds,*
> *Our Garbage Cans salute the rising sun*
> *And midday finds their work is still not done!*
> *Our railway stations make the stranger cringe.*
> *Our noises reason will in time unhinge.*
> *Homewards at night we'd ride in ladies' laps*
> *Did Tom and Nature give not arms, and Straps!*
> *But why try tell the things with which we're curst;*
> *You're "Sons of Newark" and you know the worst.*

He had what the Scots would call a pawky humor. It
had a sly touch to it. When it broke into his conversation
his eyes were lighted by a quizzical expression that was
almost a twinkle. And it was his eyes not his mouth that

smiled. He was mischievous with a straight face. His humor could take the sting out of his own difficulties. The articulate man can make a sort of confessional out of his own mind and gain relief from his troubles by giving them expression in words, finding in verbal mastery an antidote to his defeat by events. His triumph is all the more complete when he adds humor to clarity. So when Dana was convalescing from a serious operation in St. Vincent's Hospital in 1922 he sent a piece of verse to Franklin P. Adams and *The Conning Tower*. It began

> *I cannot laugh, I cannot sneeze*
> *I cannot cough, and for mine ease,*
> *I cannot even blow my nose;*
> *Aye, deeper still my burden goes,*
> *For hiccoughs pain tho' wont to please.*
> *I cannot laugh.*

IV

When he went on journeys he was a prodigious letter writer. The Newark papers received regular accounts of the places he visited and what he observed. In 1908, accompanied by Mrs. Dana, he revisited Europe. "I left Newark April 4 and returned on June 27—80 days. I was on the ocean 14 days; on railways part of 11 days; in Rouen 1, Paris 17, Tours 4, Carcassonne 2, Nimes 2, Nice 3, Rome 6, Venice 5, Florence 5, Perugia 1, Como 4, Lucerne 4, Basle 1." He visited many of the libraries but found them mainly old buildings designed for other than library purposes, housing collections of rare and ancient volumes used solely by students and by very few of them. His visits to the schools left him feeling that they had little to suggest to American public schools. He bought few books, but he did make a point of getting some desirable editions of his beloved Horace. He also brought back a few

engravings and books about engraving to supplement the
library's collection. His general comment was: "My only
regret about this trip is that I did not take it before! Short
as it was and hurried as was my view of a few only of the
things the world has talked of for centuries past, I saw
enough to put a new interest and a new meaning into
much I have read. Also, I gained, of course, a new view
of America and its opportunities and limitations and ad-
vantages."

His letters to the *Newark Sunday Call* were as varied as
his own interests. In Paris he found no yellow journals but
newsstands and booksellers everywhere. He praised France
for its railway stations with squares and parks about them,
and commented that they put the Jersey Central to blush.
The busy picture of women making every waterway a
laundry entranced him for he found the banks lined with
kneeling figures a sight that delighted his eyes. Old Florence took his thoughts by contrast to new Denver, and as
he compared them he thought both had their errors of
taste. On the whole, he considered the Renaissance artists
overestimated, and many of the old Masters praised beyond their due.

This group of letters is balanced by another series describing a trip to the West and Alaska. As he left the East
he felt its provincialism dropping from him. The journey
through the heart of the continent freed him from that
preoccupation with the magic of New York that so easily
becomes an obsession, and his letters became expansive and
optimistic with the dimensions of the mountains and the
great rivers. As he travelled from Seattle to Tacoma the
greatness of what he saw lifted him to enthusiasm: "Then
we felt the magnificence of this new land, the inland seas,
the great rivers, the mountains, the endless forests, the
valleys fertile beyond belief, and began to feel the future

as our fellow citizens will fashion it. Here is an empire which needs no imperialism, for it rules itself; can have no barriers to its trade; asks for no great armies for protection; calls out industry, skill and genius by its opportunities, and invites man by climate, scenery and established social order."

He wrote that he could not answer the question "What is Alaska like?" because it is "big enough to be like a lot of things. It is warm and cold. It has plains and mountains, great rivers and land-locked seas. It has forests and great open plains." But with all it has, "Alaska sorely needs libraries. A little more sunshine, and a few Carnegie libraries, with lively young women as librarians, would make this empire of ours a perfect delight!"

A rather morbid irony attaches to one letter that he wrote during the European trip. It was dated on the very day that the *Titanic* sank, and describes what Dana on board another ship was finding troublesome: "There are some things we don't like on this ship, and I may as well name the worst at once. The trouble is with the view. This view, for all continuous sitters and for nearly all promenaders, is limited to the sides of lifeboats that fortify the whole deck. It is very pleasant to know that if the ship goes down most of us can float about a while in small boats before we starve to death; but why should salvation be thrust upon us when what we want is view?" Values are relative. The view was not as important as lifeboats elsewhere that day.

V

Dana played golf regularly, but when he was asked his favorite recreation he named reading. His work, although with books, allowed no time for it during the working day, so he read steadily at home, or wherever or whenever he could catch a moment's time. But recreation is a misleading term to use if it implies pleasure as distinguished from drudgery, for by his own testimony: "My library and museum have been so much a source of daily pleasure that I rarely think of them as accomplishments." He never received any salary as Director of the Museum. It was to him a labor of love and a continual source of personal joy. Beatrice Winser has carried on in the same spirit. Up to date, the Newark Museum has the unique distinction of never paying a cent of salary to its Directors.

The reading that he did was discursive. Looking back he once expressed astonishment that he had read so few of the world's great books. "For example, Sterne—I've dipped in here and there a little. Newman, hardly a page." His thirty-six years as a librarian forced him to know something of everything, and he found himself reading thousands and thousands of title pages, book catalogs, magazines, and reviews. In the prolific output of present day publishing any professional bookman has to be sternly, almost terrifyingly contemporary. The librarian cannot adopt the pose of the dainty litterateur and look at no book until it is a year old, or read an old masterpiece for every new novel that appears. He must be up to date, and Dana was. Even his own statement, however, must not be overweighted, for he knew some of the good old books extraordinarily well. The process of individual selection works among the masterpieces as well as among present works. Although he may have skipped Sterne and Newman, his intellectual roots struck deep into the soil of our traditional creative literature. He recognized this, for at seventy he said: "I was born in a Vermont village but I was raised in England. . . . I mean that the opinions, the ideas about life, that I gathered during all my growing years, . . . were of English origin and came to me in books written by Englishmen. . . . They have always been to me the most interesting and seemingly the most important of all the things that have come into my life. My life has been interesting to me—in what we may call the biographical meaning of the word—not by reason of the persons I have known, but by reason of the ideas I have met, considered, enjoyed, approved, discarded, conversed and played with. . . . As for me, as I look back, I see myself surrounded by books of English birth."

Finding his satisfaction in ideas, he naturally gave little attention to accumulating money. He held that it was absurd for a young man to enter library work unless he was attached to his fellow-men. "If he is purely a maker of things or seeks only money he does not belong. He must have a sympathetic spirit and a love of the community." In a letter written to his old college friend, W. D. Parkinson, two years before he died, he said quite simply: "I have no use for my money—what little I have—and I want to get it as nearly all spent as I dare before I come to the end of things. Isn't that a good idea?" By the same token he was not greatly impressed by those whose sole claim to honor was their accumulation of money. His enthusiasms were well insulated against both the glittering and the gilded.

While he held fast to the practical ideals of his early training his natural skepticism set him apart from all forms of orthodox religion. He rarely expressed himself publicly on the subject, for he had learned it to be so full of emotional explosives that most people cannot discuss it rationally, and he was not one who took delight in heat without illumination. He recognized the church as an institution that would continue, but thought that social forces would modify its practices to take it out of the stage of habitual observance of certain forms and ceremonies to one more definitely marked by social fellowship devoted to social advance. His theological dilemma he once thoughtfully expressed in a comment on Bishop Gore's book, "Belief in God." It is highly discerning, for it puts its finger on the basic limitation of the concept of personality with which personalists of all stripes have not adequately dealt. Personality is a restrictive term not an inclusive one. We cannot use it as we can a word like "universe" to include many varieties of events and objects within it. It is something in itself apart from other things and looks or moves upon them from within its own consciousness. To call God a person is to impose this tightness upon him, and so to limit him. Dana saw this, and expressed it:

To me it is not only most presumptuous but also quite irrational for us to try to explain the universe; and, specifically, to explain it, by assuming that the somewhat behind it is a personality whose qualities are known to us, is to mislead and commit ourselves to serious errors of conduct. Personality is something which comes to us only in terms of our own experience. We of this tiny planet have a vague consciousness of it—that consciousness having, as one of its basic elements limitations and differences; and the personality of God must have the same elements. It is not a last word in creation, so far as we know—in fact something far higher may be found in other worlds,—and to ascribe it to that which may be behind all things is to trifle with the eternal, to belittle what we cannot comprehend, to make a god little more lofty than that of the most primitive of men, and to open the door to all sorts and kinds of doctrines, theories, creeds, dogmas and fanaticisms.

In spite of his own position, he held that every individual has a right to work out his philosophy in his unique way, so, during the years when he was bringing up his nephew, he sent him regularly to Sunday School.

VI

As the years wore on he had the satisfaction of seeing both his institutions win that popular following which he prized, and himself acknowledged leader in his city and his profession. Tributes from varied sources made him aware of how, often unconsciously, his influence was widely felt. The *New York Sun*, as early as 1913, praised him in its editorial columns:

Once a month for more than a year the Newark Public Library has sent *The Sun* its bulletin, *The Newarker*, and from it we have got the notion that John Cotton Dana does a good many things for his city besides presiding adequately over a large collection of books. If there is any public or private enterprise that he does not make the institution he manages help along, it must be of no importance. If there is any intellectual appetite of the townsfolk that the library does not seek to appease, it is not worthy of encouragement.

Even more emphatic was an editorial in the *Post Standard* of Syracuse:

What the word Bartlett is to the pear, the word Concord to the grape, the word Webster to dictionaries and oratory, such in a sense is the word Dana to libraries. This is because Mr. Dana, to an extent far surpassing others, has made his library an agency for democratic public welfare. He is not encumbered by professional etiquette, he makes his library help business, he abjures red tape, he goes in for the real thing.

When Stephen Graham, an Englishman who tramped through the United States, wrote "With Poor Immigrants In America," he had this sentence in his preface: "I wish to express my thanks to J. Cotton Dana who with unsparing energy and hospitality helped me to see America as she is." Dana had no recollection of any visit with Graham prior to this publication. The impression he made on an obviously casual acquaintance, however, is further indicated by a characterization in the third chapter of the book: "There is a band of workers united in the idea of making America the most pleasant and happy place to live in that the world has ever known. I refer to those working with such Americans as J. Cotton Dana, the fervent librarian; Mr. Fred Howe . . . ; John H. Finley. . . . Jane Addams."

Even more persuasive than these tributes is a letter written by Richard C. Jenkinson, President of the Board of Trustees of the Newark Library, to a personal friend after more than twenty years of close association with Dana. He took H. G. Wells' description of Sanderson in "The Story of a Great Schoolmaster," and appropriated it as veracious for Dana. He expressed his own admiration in this way:

I am president, as you know, of the Trustees of the Library. I am also on the Executive Committee of the Museum. I am rounding out nearly thirty years on the Library Board and I was one of the "Founders" of the Museum. I have come to know Mr. Dana so well and to like him so much, and to know of his value to this city so well, that I have come to the place where I agree to most anything he proposes. . . . He has shown us how to do things, and we are doing them as he suggests.

As he won the confidence of his trustees, so also he held the admiration of his staff. One of them has caught him admirably in a naïve but honest account of her experiences:

I was young and astonishingly unaware of the privilege of working in company with him. However, whatever I lacked in respectful appreciation was more than made up in unalloyed pleasure. Gradually I grew accustomed to a chief who turned naturally from a contemplation of Chinese culture to transparent tissues for mending books.

It was an experience to go into his office close on the heels of a distinguished caller and to know that in the instant your plan or perplexity would have his entire attention. Mr. Dana listened when people spoke to him and no matter how inadequately an idea was expressed somehow he grasped it. A talk with him was an inspiration.

His kindliness in case of personal trouble is beyond expression. It existed for us all. His patience with inexperience and intolerance seems hardly credible. He was serious, stern, often severe, but never uncomfortably solemn. He was never bored and never intellectually aloof. It seemed easy and natural to laugh and joke with him. His smile is a cherished remembrance.

The *New York Times* commented editorially on the essential youthfulness of his mind in his seventieth year: "Though a veteran, he has the open-mindedness and adventurous spirit of the young."

As a girl, Dorothy Canfield Fisher used to attend the Library conventions with her father, and in later years she told Dana of her father's admiration and her own emulation:

He had the most unbounded admiration for the originality and energy of your work in Newark, and used to hold you up as an example of what could be made of library work. . . all this long before everybody else began doing it, as I rejoice to see they are doing now. I have followed all I can read of what you are doing with the greatest pride as an old friend.

During his last years, however, a recurring ailment afflicted him and his body was not as youthful as his mind; several prolonged periods of weakness necessitating hospital care made him realize that his ailment was serious. He entered St. Vincent's Hospital to submit to an operation. Although he seemed to rally from the ordeal his strength could not bring him to full recovery, and on July 21, 1929 he died. His body was taken to Woodstock where it rests beside the river in the old cemetery hallowed by the graves of his forbears.

On one of his journeys to Woodstock he had written these simple lines:

> *I tire of this Eternal green—*
> *It drips from willows and*
> *It towers unashamed*
> *In Elm and Maple;*
> *It wearies*
> *Until at last beyond it and above it*
> *Blue hills beckon the eye*
> *And promise Rest.*

Now the promise is fulfilled. And the breath of the hills of home blows softly where he sleeps.